SUCCESSFULLY LEADING
Project and Technical Teams

WORKPLACE INTELLIGENCE FOR ALL TEAM MEMBERS

DOUG RUSSELL

FOREWORD BY ERVIN (EARL) COBB
Author of "*The Official Leadership Checklist and Diary for Project Management Professionals*

Published by RICHER Press

An Imprint of Richer Life, LLC
5710 Ogeechee Road, Suite 200-175, Savannah, Georgia 31405
www.richerlifellc.com

Cover Design: RICHER Media

Volume book discounts are available for groups, companies and organizations. Contact the publisher for information and order instructions.

Successfully Leading Project and Technical Teams
Workplace Intelligence For All Team Members

Doug Russell

1. Leadership & Motivations 2. Project Management 3. Technical Project Management

(pbk : alk. Paper)

ISBN: 979-8-9928996-5-8 Paperback
ISBN: 979-8-9928996-6-5 eBook

PRINTED IN THE UNITED STATES OF AMERICA

CONTENTS

FOREWORD

A Primer for Workplace Intelligence and More

If you are looking for a book where a writer provides a general discussion of leadership skills or where an educator presents an academic view of the characteristics and qualities of individuals recognized as exemplary leaders, and you chose this book, **you will be sorely disappointed.**

Along with being an admired professional colleague, a dear friend and fellow author, Doug Russell has *genuinely been there and done that* when it comes to successfully leading project and technical teams.

In this, his third published book, Doug was committed to find a way to capture many of his *lessons-learned* and communicate them in a simple, candid, straight forward, yet meaningful fashion.

In discussions with Doug when he was in the process of drafting the early manuscript, I learned of his *vision* for his new book. He was determined to structure *"Successfully Leading Project and Technical Teams"* in such a way that the book could become a unique *leadership development primer* for those working in the Tech environment.

As Doug described it to me, *"By a primer, I envision a book which can intuitively fit into any technical and management toolkit. A book that is easy to read, connects-the-dots of the sometime complicated technical development workplace, and allows all project and technical team members to more effectively work together, and possibly, develop themselves into successful leaders of projects and technical teams."*

What I experienced in reading an early release of *"Successfully Leading Project and Technical Teams: Workplace Intelligence for All Team Members,"* was a delightful combination of sincerity, insightfulness, and ingenuity.

I was very impressed in how Doug has been able to not only recall over eighty invaluable anecdotes and to share them with such candor and yet, pack each with enjoyable dialogue and instructive nuances.

When Doug asked me to write the foreword to this particular book, I was thrilled and honored for two reasons.

First of all, I worked closely with Doug while I was the Vice President and Director of the Secure Communications Operations at Motorola's Government and Systems Technology Group over thirty-years ago.

Having become professional colleagues and then friends, I watched with admiration how Doug professionally morphed over the years into a very successful and respected leader of both corporate as well as governmental projects and technical teams. For context, Doug brilliantly shares some of his major projects in Appendix A of the book.

Secondly, I am now even more impressed with Doug's ingenuity as an accomplished author. In this book, his craftiness to capture, share, and analyze the essence of what developmental experts now call *Workplace Intelligence,* as it relates to today's Tech workplace and development environments, is mystifying.

By *Workplace Intelligence*, I am referring to the comprehensive framework of cognitive, emotional, social, cultural, and political insights essential for navigating complex professional environments, as well as for thriving in modern work settings filled with challenging personalities, surprising motives, and leaders of many different flavors.

In this regard, within *"Successfully Leading Project and Technical Teams"* Doug has packed a huge amount of workplace intelligence and more into what is also a fun, enjoyable and meaningful read.

Well, Mr. Russell. Your new book clearly meets and exceeds your vision. From my view, *"Successfully Leading Project and Technical Teams"* is a ground breaking literary accomplishment, and I am sure the readers of your new book will agree.

Earl

Ervin (Earl) Cobb is a retired corporate executive and the author of 18 published books and over 100 articles, including "*The Official Leadership Checklist and Diary for Project Management Professionals*" and *"Driving Ultimate Project Performance: Transforming from Project Manager to Project Leader."*

Why This Book Might Be for You

Leaders aren't born; they are made. And they are made just like anything else—through hard work.
—Vince Lombardi, football coach

This book is meant for two main groups. First, leaders of creative technical teams down in the trenches of the organization, be they frustrated long timers or new leaders, struggling against the forces arrayed against them. Second, the students in university technical programs, be they engineering, computer science, or physics students, who someday will lead or work on technical teams.

I have heard from so many people over my thirty-five year career just how terrible the management/leadership is in their organizations. I am convinced many of the senior managers are not aware of just how destructive and demotivating their leadership actually is. That's why this book exists.

Typically, leadership jobs in tech are the reward of being good at your technical job. But doing your job well certainly does not automatically make you a good leader. And that's the rub.

Many senior tech managers think leadership is just telling people what to do, that controlling them is all that is necessary. This might work in certain combat situations, but is exactly the wrong idea on how to lead creative people.

I started out that way, as a micromanaging and controlling engineer. The same may apply to you. But ultimately, I became something very different, a leader who was appreciated by those he helped and someone who could improve business results. You can learn to do the same.

In truth, only the team itself grants you the role of leader. Otherwise, you are just one of various forms of irritation. Someone may be called the manager or leader, but if they don't learn to act as leaders, their teams will never truly follow them.

Over the years I have observed the same bad management behaviors over and over again. I've come to the conclusion that a lot of these actions are taken because nothing else occurred to them at the time. On a moment-to-moment basis almost everyone (there are always a few exceptions) tries to do the right thing.

But they often haven't been trained or informed with ideas that help them actually lead, as opposed to telling others what to do. And they never observed anyone doing it right. I'll show you how.

Maybe you feel a bit over your head trying to lead tech people. You know just telling them what to do isn't right, but what other option is there? I am sure many of you already have the underlying skills needed to be effective leaders. This book will help you bring them out.

These skills are not widely taught. They certainly weren't taught to me in my undergraduate EE program and there was just a bit in the top ten business school where I got my MBA. Outside of military officers, I've never run across anyone who was taught how to be a good leader.

I've worked with all sorts of teams, and while there will be examples from manufacturing and hardware teams, this book is meant mainly for leaders of tech development or design teams.

There are many improvement processes. They are all good processes and can be used to provide successful and profitable change. So why aren't they more effective?

I believe something is missing. That something is someone explaining, with simple and real-world stories, how to actually be successful as a team leader, regardless of the improvement process being used. If that sounds interesting, then this book is for you.

I scan the business/leadership book shelves occasionally. The number of books on leadership is huge, and many of them are great books. But the findings are sparse for one particular type of business/leadership book. That is, books that show people how they can simply implement improvements down in the trenches where they work, with a set of values that enable them to lead as well as stories on pitfalls to watch out for along the way. This book seeks to do just that.

Many of the books on the leadership shelves are high-level and written by non-engineers, people who weren't present on the tech battlefield if you will. Thus, the anecdotes are often not their own. In other words, they weren't involved in the ongoing day-to-day process of making it happen. That's where I come in. I've been there.

There is a seemingly endless list of courses you can take on the subject of leadership and leading teams, but when people actually go back to the workplace how many can successfully implement what they heard? When I search the internet, I consistently see failure rates in the 50-70% range. I want to help you return to your workplace and implement those processes successfully.

I wrote this book to try to help anyone who finds themselves in a similar situation to mine when I started, in a leadership role wondering what to do next.

As simple as that. Let's get started.

ACKNOWLEDGEMENTS

I want to thank my wife Anne Russell for being my alpha reader, able to understand what I meant rather than what I wrote, helping me to cut useless marble from the statue, as it were.

Also, beta readers Laura Stein and Leslie Martinich provided comments that gave a different perspective from my own and helped me tighten and improve the book. Earl Cobb suggested a title change that helped resolve a question I had wrestled with for way too long.

I want to thank the RICHER Press Publishing Team for their publishing guidance and expertise.

Finally, I want to thank the quote givers in *"What People Say,"* and all the thousands of folks I worked with over the years. It was a gas. Thank you all!

PROLOGUE

"Leadership sometimes means you need to look inside yourself for motivation and inspiration. Or you can find personal inspiration from someone who has been there, done that, and done it well."—Jeff Haden, Inc. Magazine article

"A good leader needs to have a compass in his head and a bar of steel in his heart." —Robert Townsend, best-selling author and executive

Over my thirty-five plus year career I never had a team building or designing something that failed to meet its business goals. That's right. **Never.** See Appendix A for the list of major projects throughout my career, with the names changed to protect the innocent and so as not to get sued by the guilty.

I emphasize the word "business" because in the beginning, I didn't always do well with the actual people I led. ("Zealot Failure" in Chapter 2 relates those events).

But I learned. This book is meant to help you do the same. **I want this book to be the most useful book ever written about effective leadership down in the trenches of an organization.**

I led hardware engineering, software engineering, manufacturing, business, and project management teams in the semiconductor, defense, and software industries. I also taught the principles in this book as a consultant to a top State Farm Insurance agent and his team, a contact lens maker, an Iridium phone vendor, a defense software company, and a software start-up, among others.

And I've used these techniques with middle school basketball teams, the toughest customers of all. In all, twenty and a half out of twenty-one notable projects were successful at meeting their stated organizational goals.

Along the way I was well rewarded for my efforts, but businesses—due to their essential natures—restricted the reach of my creativity. Before I left the steady paycheck world in 2008 to become a team leadership consultant, I tried out several ideas with large numbers of audiences in the corporate world.

In 2011, the American Management Association published my first book, *Succeeding in the Project Management Jungle: How to Manage the People Side of Projects.* The book hit #8 on the Amazon Project Management best-sellers list for about fifteen minutes. The broad impact needed to make a real difference did not materialize. As one client put it, *"Your stuff is great one-on-one, but it's a bit cerebral and came off kind of abstract in your (first) book."*

Over the years since my first book was published, I've further refined my ideas. I led an IEEE Engineering Management Society chapter; spoke to an engineering management convention at West Point, a State Farm Agents Sectional Meeting, chapters of IEEE, PMI, Rotary Club International, International Institute of Business Analysts; and taught team leadership to several small companies.

Many people came up after my talks. Almost to a person they would say something like, "You must have worked in my company. It's just like that there!" They poured out story after story of how bad their experiences had been inside technical teams.

Not surprising. After all, the overall global process-improvement market is projected by worldmetrics.org to reach $24.2 billion in 2025.

That's a lot of money and shows someone thinks things need improving!

The US, as the largest world economy, likely accounts for roughly between 35–40% of the process-improvement market; placing the U.S. total spending in the range of $8.5 – $10 billion annually.

Yet. Only 30–40% of technical projects fully meet their goals.

Why you ask? Well, here's why.

- 50% are challenged (partially meet objectives but overrun time/cost); and
- *"Only 10% of knowledge workers teams are high performing,"* per Susan Lucia Annunzio, in her book *Contagious Success.*

This is staggeringly poor performance considering the stakes and effort involved. I believe these numbers. It's a mess out there.

Over the years I often discussed the reactions of audiences and the poor project success rate with other people. Some were my peers. Others were my employees, my direct managers, layers above my direct manager, and other involved people. A friend summed it up best at lunch one day.

He said: *"People who get to be senior managers in engineering organizations inside tech companies share a lot of common traits. They almost always, of course, are engineers. Engineering school is hard and requires focus and problem-solving skills to excel. Most engineering students are thus quiet and hardworking. Generally, they don't relate well to people. So, when they are eventually thrust into leadership roles, they don't really know how to act. Or how to lead. And they make a lot of the same kinds of mistakes. Over and over and over again."*

I was able to help many teams and many individuals, but I've written this book to reach a broader audience of the people who need to know more about leading tech and other teams effectively.

This is a leadership book, not a project management book, although of course projects are central to everything I write. Leadership can be taught, if the person is interested.

Maybe some leaders are born—I couldn't really say—but I know leadership can be learned. I'm living proof. I'm going to show you what I did to evolve into an effective leader, and how it can work for you.

I've been working off and on for several years on various formats and structures for this book. I've always felt Robert Townsend's classic *Up the Organization*, with its structure of short, concise, funny, and on target stories was a great format for many of the same management issues that bothered, and continue to bother me, many years after Townsend's book was first published.

This book has eighty-seven concise stories in three parts:

- **Leadership.** What is effective leadership and what is poor leadership.
- **Culture.** What constitutes a successful culture and how to implement it.

- **Process of Working with Management and Teams.** How to successfully lead your teams, implement your own unique culture, and how to understand and work with the individuals on your teams and in your management.

I hope this book helps you to become the effective leader you can and want to be.

PART ONE

This section is based on the question how can you successfully lead anything if you don't know what leadership actually is?

We define effective leadership vs poor leadership, and ask you to think about your personal viewpoint on leadership.

We build on that thinking with some experiences in my youth that influenced my ultimate leadership approach. These are to help you kick-start your thinking on leadership.

We explore what effective leaders and poor leaders think, say, and do. Then the importance of continuous learning follows and how change is necessary but must be structured properly as well as aligned to the team.

The section finishes up with the concept that much success is found in learning from failure. I share my biggest failure and what I learned from it.

Many people have spoken on the importance of failure. My favorite quote is that of George Clooney, the famous actor, the nephew of Rosemary Clooney. Her rock star-like status made him feel small when he began acting. George Clooney said, *"There's nothing you learn from success. You learn everything from failing, and fear of failing is what holds people back from doing anything."*

CHAPTER ONE

Leadership – The Concept

Leadership is the quality and character that determines the performance, the results.
—Frances Hesselbein, author, CEO, Girl Scouts of America and Chairman of the Peter Drucker Foundation

Leadership is influence; Leadership is empathy.
—John C Maxwell, author, speaker, and pastor

Leadership is unlocking people's potential to become better.
—Bill Bradley, basketball player and author

Leadership is an action verb, and touches every aspect of our lives, our relationships, and our professions.
— Ervin (Earl) Cobb, CEO and author of seventeen best-selling books on leadership

In my experience few people understand leadership. **Instead, most managers think their job is to control people.** Over-control is the essence of what poor management is all about.

These types of managers think what I'm going to tell you in this book is "soft" stuff. They say, "Just tell 'em what to do and make sure they do it! How hard that can be?" I've heard statements like this so many times.

Of course, effective leadership is not controlling and telling people what to do, and it is not doing their thinking for them. Instead, effective leadership enables teams to do their work better, quicker, and more unified as a unit. This is especially true in creative work, such as software coding and engineering development.

There are thousands of books, hundreds of companies, and who knows how many executive coaches and training classes all trying to improve leadership. The specific actions needed to lead a platoon of soldiers versus those needed for a CEO's staff are of course different (one size does not fit all) but there are things in common in leading all teams.

Fair enough, you say, but what is leadership? The four quotations at the beginning of this chapter work for me. You should come up with your own statement of what leadership is to you.

My personal definition is "Leadership is the ability to help a team meet its commitment to the organization, in such a way that the individuals and the team grow towards their personal and professional goals."

To do this, think about what leadership means to you. Really give it some thought. Research quotes on the word leadership. Maybe some or all of the quotes from the start of the chapter resonate with you. Maybe not. Read more about the authors of quotes you like and see where those threads take you.

How Leadership Feels

Leadership starts with self. You must know yourself really well, know your emotional responses and the impact they're going to have, indirectly, on people.
—Shannon O' Flaherty, healer and spiritual coach

Examine every word of Shannon O' Flaherty's statement above. Her quote lines up perfectly with my approach to leadership.

Let's break her quote down into three phrases: Know yourself; know your emotional responses; and know how they indirectly impact people. Think deeply about all three of those phrases and how they make you feel about leadership.

What follows are my attempt at explaining how leadership feels for me. The bullets focus on each of the three phrases.

Know Yourself

Leadership is Lonely.
—Kobe Bryant, 18-time All-Star basketball player

There is surprisingly little written about leadership being lonely and the impact that has on self.

- **High Pressure to perform and meet expectations**. This is actually a desired state. I am a highly competitive person who has always been drawn to the stress of competition in sports and business. I automatically kept score in all our neighborhood games as a kid, searched the box scores in the newspaper to see how my favorite teams did, and was the first parent to yell "put up the points," if the scorekeeper for our children's schools' teams forgot to do so.

  I simply don't get enough of an adrenaline rush if I am not striving for something difficult. Leadership may not be the right job for people who don't like to compete. You decide if it's right for you.

- **Peer Isolation.** As a leader in the trenches, you have few peers. Senior management, above you, generally are just pushing for results and their next promotion. Your equals in other departments view you with suspicion as a competitor and a threat. The people under you are often trying to curry favor and some are looking for the opportunity to knock you off.

- **Empathy Required.** The ability to truly understand a situation from the other person's viewpoint is empathy. As Dr. Joseph W. Walker, III says, *"Empathy allows us to lead with compassion rather than condemnation."*

  I actually don't care much for conflict, but feel a strong desire for the best outcome to be realized, and that the truth be identified. If you hate conflict and lack empathy, you better learn how to compensate or this issue may be a showstopper for you as a leader.

- **Second-guessing past decisions.** This one can be tough, the so-called yips of leadership. Like the yips in golf, second guessing past decisions can hurt your confidence, lower your enthusiasm and overall energy level (your joie de vivre). This is why you need a bedrock set of standards, that is, a culture (See Part II) that you apply to every action you take and decision you make. It will give you solace when the day-to-day events and setbacks challenge you and will temper your exuberance when you succeed.

Know Your Emotional Responses

- **Conflict Management**. It's a drag refereeing various team member's "disputes" about issues that come up. Due to family dynamics, I learned at a very young age to see both sides of most situations and this certainly helped me to do the same as a leader.

- **Lack of Support**. In the business and tech world, a huge portion of many people's emotional incentive at work comes from being part of a system, a group, a tribe. The type of change agent mindset that is required for an innovative leader means you will receive resistance—overt and covert—from many directions. This often feels like lack of support and can drain your energy level and positive outlook.

- **Social Affirmation.** Famous football coach Knute Rockne said, *"Leaders are like eagles, they don't tend to flock."* It helps if you are confident in yourself, so that you don't need much social affirmation. Fortunately, that was my situation. And you can learn to affirm yourself. Having a loving spouse and family has also been a bedrock of support and comfort.

Indirect Impact on Others

- **Burden of the Culture.** As I will go into more later, the leader is the person who creates the culture and ultimately, sees that things get done. That's what the famous President Truman quote, *"the buck stops here,"* means. Same point for, *"no easy problems reach this desk,"* from President Eisenhower.

  A strong happy feeling of the impact I have been able to make on the overall organization's success and the better work environment I've been able to create, perhaps only for a limited time, for the people on my team was a key motivator for me.

General Douglas MacArthur said, *"A true leader has the confidence to stand alone, the courage to make tough decisions, and the compassion to listen to the needs of others."*

I really like his last phrase for its emphasis on listening to others. To close the loop on Kobe Bryant's quote above, this is why leadership is not so lonely to me. The connection with others, when I understand them and see that they get that fact, is truly inspirational. The feeling is sublime, even better than the perfect pass (not shot) in a basketball game.

"The engineering schools certainly don't teach leadership."

Leadership Life Learning

Good enough, you might say. So *how* does a person learn to be a leader of teams?

The engineering schools certainly don't teach leadership. Some of them have a few leadership courses, but as far as I can tell there is as much pain and stress in the engineering workforce as there ever was. Team assignments, while sometimes useful (and sometimes not), are not the solution.

A few suggestions:

- Think about times when you were in a leadership position, be it in school, on the playground or ball fields, or a youth activity. How did it go? How did it feel? What did you do and say? Most importantly, what did you learn? Write these examples down.
- Think about your parents, siblings, friends, teachers, coaches, leaders from youth activities, or others. Which of those individuals demonstrated qualities useful for the kind of leadership you want to do? What were the results of their actions and statements? What did you learn from them? Write those examples down. Pure gold for your future team culture!

Briefly, here is a synopsis of what most influenced me.

Two parents who served others in many things they did. For example, my dad, while working full time in a high-pressure job, coached our church league softball team, and helped the team to become champions. My mom rode herd on the neighborhood kids, receiving profuse thanks from the working moms.

Determination was learned from observing my dad; Empathy was learned from my mom.

"The Bottom Line is you should learn about leadership from your parents, friends, and whoever else has shown that quality to you."

Youthful Leadership

An example of youthful leadership success that clearly showed me the power of listening to my team came in an MBA class case study called "Looking Glass." The class was split into two teams of something like six to eight people. Each team "ran" a business. The corporate officers and the CEOs were to be appointed by the professor. Each person was assigned their own conference room as an office. We were then told the business details of our hypothetical companies.

The prof announced the two CEOs. I was one of them, to the obvious surprise of my ultra-competitive, mostly marketing and finance-oriented MBA classmates. The other CEO was New York bound. She gave me a contemptuous non-glance and the exercise began.

We went to our assigned offices (conference rooms) where further individualized sealed written instructions awaited. I read my instructions, something about "working with my staff to solve the business question as quickly as possible." There was a relatively short time limit, thirty to forty-five minutes comes to mind.

After a minute or so, I hopped up and started a circuit of my "staff's" offices. I sat down with each of them, and asked them what they knew. Finally, I went back to my office and collated my notes. I wrote down our answer to the business question, then went back to the classroom. My team showed up. We waited.

The deadline arrived. The other team showed up, angry looks on their faces. They had nothing, whereas the professor congratulated our team for correctly solving the problem. We had won, with effective Team Leadership being the point of the exercise.

The other CEO had stayed in her office waiting for her team to come to her. Her staff never efficiently transmitted their personal information to anyone. She and her team made it very clear that they thought the exercise was stupid.

From this I learned that I had the right instincts to effectively lead teams in a competitive business situation, simulation though it was.

This increased my confidence.

What are your own nascent leadership examples?

The Bottom Line: Learn about leadership from your parents, friends, and whoever else has shown that quality to you. In Chapter 2, I will cover leaders in the working world.

CHAPTER TWO

Leaders Good and Bad

In this chapter we're going to cover the differences in how effective leaders and poor leaders think, speak, and act, as well as how they view change and continuous learning.

Effective Leaders

The greatest leaders mobilize others by coalescing people around a shared vision.
—Ken Blanchard, author of The One-Minute Manager, speaker, and business consultant

The bad leader is he who the people despise; the good leader is he who the people praise; the great leader is he who the people say, "We did it ourselves.
—Peter M. Senge, author of The Fifth Discipline

Great leaders are almost always great simplifiers who can cut through argument, debate, and doubt to offer a solution everybody can understand.
—Gen. Colin Powell, diplomat, and Chairman of the US Joint Chiefs of Staff

Leadership cannot just go along to get along.
—Jesse Jackson, civil rights activist, politician, and ordained minister

"There were many other good bosses, but these are the effective leaders I was most influenced by."

Effective Leaders in My Career

During my thirty-five-year career, there were a few leaders who influenced me the most. One was a bluff Harvard evening school educated, innovative manufacturing leader who had a soft spot for the workers and a worker's disdain for engineers and managers. From him, **my appreciation for transparency grew**.

The second leader who influenced me greatly was smart (MSEE from Arizona State), a deal maker, businessman, and never harsh (highly unusual in that corporation). From him I learned the effectiveness of a softer **communication approach**. He was the best person I know able to balance the political skills required at senior levels (he ultimately became a CEO elsewhere) along with the people skills required to effectively lead, not control, his teams.

My leadership style owes much to those two men.

The final person who made a significant positive impact, not so much in my leadership style, but in my career in general, had many years before been the design leader of Motorola's MC68000 microprocessor which went into the Apple Mac and many more computers.

He trusted and approved my approach when I first joined his organization. With so much resistance from those lower down in his organization, it is **his trust, earned after just a one-hour meeting, that increasingly stands out as the years roll by.**

At the time, I just assumed it would happen. The confidence of youth.

The leader who most influenced my team leadership approach (from afar) is Coach Mike Krzyzewski at Duke University, which was in a long basketball slump when he was hired those oh so many years ago. As his program became relevant and loved, then dominant and hated, I watched it all. I read his books. I even got to attend a practice, where the communication of twelve players was incredibly loud!

I watched his style as he coached collegians, then Olympians. All successes. Might sound odd, but I found many similarities with how he led basketball teams and how I wanted to lead technical teams.

Here's what I observed and implemented in my own way on successful teams.

- **No micro management**. Let the players play; don't draw up a lot of complicated plays they have to remember. I made sure the processes I added, such as schedules, metrics, and so forth helped to solve my team's problems.
- **Build leaders on the floor**. He has often said several of his easiest coaching years were when he had Christian Laettner, because the team members were more scared of Laettner than they were of Coach K. That's saying something. I looked for leadership potential and worked with the individuals to help them be better leaders.
- **Manage the motivation and structure of the team**. Often noted as "not an X's and O's guy," instead Coach K watched and listened to his players. He had exit interviews at the end of each season to discuss each player's strengths and areas for improvement. Although I couldn't hold a candle technically to my creative experts, I watched and listened. I found out the issues that needed fixing and got them fixed.
- **Identify and communicate unique roles for each player,** based on the player's skills and what the team needs. Can a great shooter win a basketball game without a rebounder or a point guard? Nope. A design engineer is extremely valuable, but so is the Verification or Test person. Just different roles. I made sure each function was truly listened to.
- **Trust and Communication** are the two critical team values, as Coach K writes in his book *Leading with the Heart.* I would add Accountability, Transparency, and Integrity, as shown in Chapter 3, to my bedrock set of values.

There were many other good bosses, but these are the effective leaders I was most influenced by. Now, let's turn to the broader questions of what leaders think, do, and say.

What an Effective Leader Thinks

If you think you can do a thing, or think you can't do a thing, you are right.
—Henry Ford, Genius

An effective leader sees their team as individuals, each with their own unique strengths and weaknesses. They think thoughts like, *what help/tools does Jose need to improve?* Or *what does the older worker, Bob, need to overcome his bluntness?* Or *how to help Betty, who is quiet, but a natural born leader?*

To the employees involved, these actions by the effective leader are *helpful,* not controlling or negative. They also are good for the business profit margin and build team esprit de corp.

The Bottom Line: Effective leaders always think of their team members as assets to be valued and work to enable them to grow.

"The Bottom Line is that effective leaders truthfully say what needs to be said, when its needed, in order to help their teams succeed."

What an Effective Leader Says

An Effective Leader:

- **Will come through the workplace almost daily** at a minimum to interact with employees and to be seen. To be available. The timing of these trips needs to emerge naturally, and not feel staged.
- **Asks "How's it going?"** seriously, listens to the response, and, as appropriate, acts upon what is said. Also, the effective leader gauges team member's body language and state of mind as they approach them. Be sensitive to wasting your team member's time. A simple "hi" in passing to someone hunched over their workbench often works just as well as a conversation and positive eye contact.
- Poor leaders don't do this. They say things like, *"Oh, I don't want to bother them, let them work."* What they really mean is *"I don't want to be bothered,"* and you better believe that the workers soon know that.
- **Never talks negatively to one employee about other employees**. Save those things, if you must, for your spouse or friend, whoever is your trusted confidant. They don't want to hear it either, though!
- **Answers all questions honestly and transparently**, especially touchy ones like business outlook or potential layoffs.
- **Doesn't make "profit" the first word** to come out of their mouth. After all, is winning the first thing out of a basketball coach's mouth? Everyone knows winning is the goal, just like everyone knows profit is why the business is there.
- **Finds a positive way to say what needs to be said**, but also gives bad news straight. The key here is that the employees will know they are being told the truth, that nothing they need to know is being kept from them.

- **Praises the team**. On one large factory project I held weekly "Find Somebody Doing Something Right," stand up meetings at 1PM on Fridays. Employees would nominate others who had done something useful for them or the project that week. After the meeting was finished, so long as we had met the week's work goals, the team could leave early!
- **Shares a handful of key metrics** at periodic team meetings (monthly or quarterly). Employees are interested in such things as "Are we doing better or worse than we were?" or "The special weekend sale we had two weeks ago worked great. We cleared X% of the inventory!"
- **Watches and listens** to their audience as they present information and changes their approach- and even the items discussed- to improve audience interest, so as to not waste their employees' time. It is not *your* time to waste.

The Bottom Line: Effective leaders truthfully say what needs to be said, when its needed, in order to help their teams succeed.

What an Effective Leader Does

A leader is not an administrator who loves to run others, but someone who carries water for his people so that they can get on with their jobs.
—Robert Townsend, best-selling author, and executive

Leadership is not just you thinking about it, but you actually doing something about it.
—Ervin (Earl) Cobb, CEO and author of *Becoming Transformational Leaders in the Post-Biden Era: Leveraging Visioning, Veracity, and Vocalization*

Listening is essential. You must assume employees, management, and customers see and interpret every action you take, and if you don't listen, you'll lose their commitment to you.

An Effective Leader:

- **Knows their every action needs to be geared towards making others better**, and the overall team thus more effective. In every act, an effective leader shows their values and how they are aligned to meeting the team's and organization's goals.
- **Listens with feeling** as they "walk about" with the team. This builds trust if done properly. My first major project (see "Zealot Failure" later in this chapter) was a financial success, but was a people failure **because I didn't listen**. I knew a lot of things, but not about what my team knew. **A good leader should speak only about 15-25% of the time.**
- Even then, they should be **asking questions and checking the temperature of the team members** (feeding back to them what was heard and getting their agreement or correction with what was said.)
- **Delegates everything possible to where the work actually gets done**. This allows the leader to be available for emerging problems, to identify and mitigate risks, and to spend as much time as possible not putting out fires.

- This delegation also allows growth from within the organization, with employee satisfaction and benefits to the business in terms of quick decision making. This is akin to how and why the US Army pushes tactical decisions (not strategic) down to the performing unit.

The Bottom Line: An effective leader spends time listening to their teams, and looks for problems that the team needs to be fixed so they can be successful.

Making Decisions: Three Things Can Happen

Courage and confidence lead to decision making.
–Mike Krzyzewski, 5 NCAA basketball championships, six gold medals as head coach of the US Men's National Team

I did a cooperative education internship program when I was an undergraduate. In a "co-op" program you alternate semesters at school with semesters at work.

Getting advice from senior managers was part of the experience I gained. The chief engineer at the huge paper mill I worked for* took time from his busy schedule to talk with me.

He was all about work, very grim and strong. Had a resemblance to the actor Anton Lesser. He once told me how important it was to make timely decisions when I got out into the work force.

He said three things can result when a big problem lands in your lap and a potentially costly decision has to be made.

"First," he said, *"you can do nothing. That rarely works; generally, the situation festers and just gets worse."*

"Second, you can see you made a mistake and try again to fix it."
"Third, you can do something that solves the problem. Bravo," he said, *"What could be better?"*

"Isn't solving problems what engineers do?" I asked quizzically. *"That's what we do, right? It's why we're learning all this calculus and electrical engineering theory? To help us to learn problem-solving skills?"*

"You'd be surprised," he said. *"Most engineering types tend to be perfectionists. Making no decision is better for them sometimes than taking a chance on a mistake."*

***Widest fourdrinier in the US for magazine paper at the time. The fourdrinier revolutionized industrial paper production. It uses a horizontal, moving screen of woven mesh or plastic to form a continuous web of paper by draining water from a pulp slurry. The web then passes through press, dryer, and calendar sections at high speed to create the final paper product. The wider and faster the fourdrinier the higher the profits.

That was the best one-on-one advice I ever got from a senior manager.

The Bottom Line: Effective leaders use the data at hand to make the best decision they can make at the time.

Effective Leaders Learn

Leadership and learning are indispensable to each other.
—John F. Kennedy, 35th President of the United States

When things go right, I read. When things go wrong, I read more.
—Sara Nelson, President of the Association (Union) of Flight Attendants

If I am through learning, I am through.
–John Wooden, coach and 10-time NCAA basketball champion

Effective Leaders are learning all the time about all sorts of things. This is a key difference from poor leaders.

Effective Leaders:

- **Generally, read broadly**. Ask your managers what they read. Chances are if their reading includes books on leadership, they are interested in getting better at the craft. If, instead, they focus on technical books, chances are they may be excellent technical people, but have little interest in leadership.
- **Attend useful or interesting courses and conferences**. They glean ideas from those sources. They talk about ideas, not other people.
- **Learn from other good leaders**. This might include parents, families, and friends as appropriate. Incorporate that learning into your approach. Also find out the best-known-methods of experts in your field and in leadership.
- **Find out who they are as individuals** and use that knowledge to grow into the leader they want to become. To do this, sage old Socrates said, *"First, know thyself."*
- **Learn from their teams**. After all, the team members know more about the day-to-day operation and details than the leader. In addition to learning about the operation, asking questions of your team builds rapport and hence trust.
- **Network** by attending PMI, IEEE, and other key professional organizations. They may also join business networking

organizations like Vistage, Business Networking International, meetup.com, Women in Business, or Rotary International. In this way they find senior managers* who are willing to give their improvement ideas a chance.

- **Plan** for the long haul, and build in natural and sincere ways to praise people.
- **They are confident** in themselves, so they don't worry about assigning blame or taking credit.
- **Own the culture** in order to execute the change that is needed.
- **Understand** their job is to facilitate the team's success. They help the team establish roles for each person that maximize that person's skills. They create a culture of continuous improvement, matched to the individual's interests and abilities.

The above listed actions are rewarding for the business in so many ways: Happier more productive employees leave less often. Profits and quality went up on every project I led in the way I describe in this book.

Continuing to learn all that you are interested in will help you. The joy is in the learning and applying it to help teams improve.

The Bottom Line: Effective leaders are all about learning, and learn to be more effective over time.

***Senior managers are people above you in the hierarchy of the organization. See Appendix D.

Poor Leaders

A bad leader can take a good plan and destroy it, while a good leader can take a bad plan and make it work.
—John C. Maxwell. author, speaker, and pastor

No man will make a great leader who wants to do it all himself, or to get all the credit for doing it.
—Andrew Carnegie, industrialist, and philanthropist

Controlling slave-drivers are endemic in tech and elsewhere in business. "Just make sure things get done around here" or words to that effect have been said to me more than once.

Some people question how much good vs poor leadership really matters. Let's explore briefly a couple of examples that graphically highlight the differences.

First, the Challenger Space Shuttle disaster, a subject that most Americans are at least somewhat aware of. The O-rings that connected sections of the engine became brittle at lower temperatures. It was much too cold for a successful launch at Cape Canaveral on the January 28, 1986, launch date. Engineers recommended the shuttle not be flown below 53°F. The low temperature in nearby Melbourne, Florida that morning was 26°F, a record low for the day which still stands 39 years later. The Space Shuttle Challenger exploded 73 seconds after liftoff.

A catastrophic failure of the O-rings caused the Space Shuttle to explode. Engineers were overridden repeatedly by management due to political pressures to show the program could launch like an assembly line product, instead of the essential flying R&D project it really was. Seven astronauts, including schoolteacher Kristie McAuliffe, died in what could hardly have been a bigger nightmare for NASA.

The key technical investigator on the Rogers Commission, Nobel prize winning physicist Richard Feynman, said *"For a successful technology, reality must take precedence over public relations, for nature cannot be fooled."*

An effective leadership team would have never launched the Space Shuttle that day. They listened to their senior management and ignored the workers whose jobs were to help apply good engineering principles that had been agreed to beforehand.

No one faced criminal charges as a result of the Challenger disaster. While several senior managers retired or were reassigned, many critics argued that the career consequences were minimal compared to the gravity of the disaster, which killed all seven astronauts aboard, gravely affecting their families, friends, and coworkers, not to mention saddening countless Americans and others around the world.

The incident led to significant organizational changes within NASA and a nearly 3-year suspension of the Space Shuttle program. The Rogers commission, charged with investigating the disaster, found that NASA's management culture and decision-making processes were major contributors to the tragedy. A damning indictment of poor management.

Another example of deliberate poor management actions that resulted in ruined lives was Enron Corporation's spectacular collapse in 2001 due to widespread corporate fraud and accounting scandals. Employees had invested heavily — in some cases exclusively — in Enron stock through their 401(k) retirement plans, which was strongly encouraged by the company. When Enron's stock price plummeted from over $90 to under $1, employees lost their retirement savings, while top executives had sold their shares earlier and walked away with millions. The collapse led to one of the largest bankruptcies in US history (at the time) and resulted in the dissolution of Arthur Andersen, one of the five largest audit and accountancy firms in the world. The passage of the Sarbanes-Oxley Act of 2002, aimed at increasing corporate accountability, is also seen as a result. Several corporate officers served prison time.

In both cases, management valued money solely over people, customer satisfaction, safety, and employee financial safety. In business school we were told repeatedly that our jobs would be to maximize *shareholder* value. Rarely mentioned was maximizing the service quality to our customers and certainly not the more amorphous phrase "serve the common good."

Next is an example of when I was a poor leader. But, unlike many, I learned. What I learned follows the story.

Zealot Failure

Success is never final; failure is never fatal. It's courage that counts.
—John Wooden, coach and 10-time NCAA basketball champion

Initial Great Success. Then Failure. Followed by an Epiphany.

This was my first leadership opportunity, just out of grad school and full of the energy of the converted.

I focused on operations management and organizational development courses, unlike the vast majority of my MBA classmates, who focused on marketing and finance.

My undergraduate degree and previous six years of experience were in electrical engineering. During a recruiting visit for an internship between MBA years, an engineering manager asked what I wanted to work on. I said *"manufacturing, because that's where the best problems are."* Surprised, (all electrical engineers should want to work in the engineering department, I guess) he passed me on to manufacturing. I interned there for the summer in Arizona then joined them upon graduation.

I became the Operations Project Leader on one of their largest production contracts. The complex hardware was in high demand, but had disappointing profits and poor quality.

I was powerfully motivated to introduce the new techniques I had learned. This was very much a possibility, as the equipment was being built in the style of Frederick Taylor's so called "scientific manufacturing," or "Theory X," which posits that employees are either workers or planners. The worker's input is not solicited; they are just there to do manual labor. Planners perform the so-called scientific side of the work, where all the decisions are made.

Workers are timed at their work (Remind you of Amazon, UPS, or a call center?), and are responsible for populating only one, or, at most, a few different board types. The thought—terribly wrong thought—was they would thus "gain efficiency" at those tasks.

In contrast, to build only what is needed, when its needed, is called a pull system. Under Theory X, the cross-training needed for such a system is viewed as unnecessary and wasteful, and since the assemblers only know how to build a few board types, they build as much as they can of those board types and just "push" the hardware downstream where it piles up, sitting around anywhere and everywhere. A mess.

I wanted to fix these problems. Fortunately, the Operations Manager for that section had been doing similar things on other projects. His name was Bob, and he was one of the two best leaders I learned from in my career.

Bob had achieved great results on a pilot project with what he called a self-regulated team approach and wanted to try the concept on my project. We later did the same for an engineering development team and we wrote a paper on what we accomplished, which was presented at a West Point conference.

Briefly, the idea was to have a cross-trained team (many people who could build many different assembly types) of empowered workers who progressively accepted—as a team—the total responsibilities and duties needed to complete a well-defined piece of work. Management (us)—with input from the team—would set goals and boundaries for the team, then help solve issues the team couldn't fix, and monitor and report progress. It worked great.

The results:

- Quality increased. Defects in assembly went down enormously as the workers began to care more about the product and appreciated being part of the solution.
- Cycle time (average time to complete a shipped unit) was reduced by approximately 75%.
- Cost per unit was reduced by 25%.
- Floor space needed was reduced by 75%.
- Inventory jumped off the shelves, saving on inventory carrying costs.
- Schedule performance increased, and became steady and predictable, a huge customer service benefit.
- Deliveries for the contract were finished several months early.

- Profits per unit improved far beyond our expectations.

A great success by anyone's measure. But, alas, all was not well. Read on for my failure. In my zeal to make change, I had listened to no one other than Bob, and I had bought into his workers vs management philosophy a bit more than was good for me.

Towards the end of the project—unbeknownst to Bob—I was locked out of the project area and a new guy I arrogantly hadn't listened to took over. The order for my removal occurred several layers above Bob. They moved me to another factory that was being converted to run four different projects with the same personnel, a great opportunity.

It wasn't exactly a demotion, although it felt like it. I felt a fair amount of shame at being dismissed from the project in that way. There was some confusion and bad politics involved; let's leave it at that. The fellow most responsible for my removal and I reconciled and are still friendly.

Along the way a kind HR person gave me a copy of the book *A Peacock in the Land of the Penguins: A Fable about Creativity and Courage.* I guess I was the peacock. More like a turkey! But this turkey learned from his failure.

The project, like all my others was successful—wildly so—as a business venture. The failure was my micromanaging, my lack of trust in others, my resistance to any ideas other than Bob's or my own, and a complete disconnect with the people.

"To feel fulfilled and useful, you have to keep score of your success, to see improvement and results."

What I Learned From Zealot Failure

The only constant in life is change. You should make sure you lead it, and not become a victim of it.
—Ervin (Earl) Cobb and Charlotte D. Grant-Cobb, authors of Living a More Thoughtful Life: Thinkable Thoughts and Relevant Reflections

I had, without paying much attention to what others said or thought, been a zealot for the needed improvements. I too slavishly followed Bob's guidance, as excellent and needed as it was.

As author Roy T. Bennett says, *"It's only after you've stepped out of your comfort zone that you begin to change, grow, and transform."* Well, I stepped outside my comfort zone and learned that I had to balance and match my zeal for improvement with the organization and people I was working with. That balance and matching process has been a part of my approach ever since.

I have great empathy for others, so I learned to mute my know-it-all persona, and realized I enjoyed listening to and getting to know people better.

I can also examine myself critically. I began to apply a process of critical self-analysis to each new opportunity that came my way.

I consciously worked to minimize my weaknesses, while at the same time maximizing my strengths.

I found sitting on a bench getting a circuit to work was boring and isolated me from the results (improvements, shipping product, winning) I found most interesting. To feel fulfilled and useful, I have to keep score of my success, to see improvement and results. Projects and teams satisfied my need for a frequent new challenge.

This approach to new learning and self-analysis set the basis for a career where my projects always met their commitments to the organization, while also improving the working lives of many employees in those organizations.

I became a leader who was appreciated by those he helped—with some of them applying the same tools in their careers—and someone who could improve business results for the organizations I worked for. You can do the same!

How a Poor Leader Thinks

The first principle is that you must not fool yourself and you are the easiest person to fool.
—Richard Feynman, Nobel prize winning physicist

Often, poor leaders view team members as "them," that is, people who aren't like "me." "Them" are people somehow different from the leader in some attribute in the poor leader's mind connected to poor performance.

The "them" could be older workers, younger workers, less educated workers, more educated workers, Southerners, Northerners, Easterners, Westerners, black people, white people, brown people, lazy, pushy, laid-back people, or all of the above. This kind of thinking leads to assumptions about the group that prevent the team and the poor leader from being successful.

For example, if a leader, call her Becky, only has a bachelor's degree in engineering, Becky might assume engineers with master's and PhD's will look down on her. Any resistance to her ideas or "orders," might therefore be viewed as disrespect, not as an honest effort to help. Or Becky may assume they are abstract thinkers, don't work hard, are hard to manage, or want too much money. These prejudices often lead to misunderstandings and arguments; impede successful communication; and ultimately impact the team's ability to succeed.

Another example might be that of an independent bookstore owner taking over a long-standing jewel in the community as her first store. Most customers and employees are older than her, let's call her Mona, by a couple of decades. Mona is motivated! After all, her own money is involved, and owning her own business, where she could take whatever actions she wanted, is something she has often dreamed of.

Mona therefore is always doing something, opening boxes, setting up displays, talking to book reps, staying busy! Mona can see the older workers in the store aren't moving as fast as she does, that they don't have her energy level. So, she may think they don't work hard, that they are there for the pay (meager as it might be), and the generous savings on books. Mona doesn't realize the women are experienced enough in life and in their work tasks that they conserve their energy. They get plenty done, they just don't have energy to waste.

The Bottom Line: Poor leaders think of their employees as commodities to be used, and not to be developed or listened to.

What a Poor Leader Says

Poor leaders reveal themselves with every statement they make. They often imply with little snippy comments that they are the only ones who work hard. They use this passive-aggressive approach to point out their concerns because they are afraid of hearing the truth.

When they hold team meetings (rarely), a bad leader talks almost the whole meeting, without much consideration for whether the information being relayed is key or even important to the employees. In the last story in Chapter 8, I discuss how to host a proper team meeting.

A bad leader often makes dismissive and derogatory statements in the office, well out of earshot of almost everyone, except the one or two "trusted" people who work in that space. Statements like "Why can't anybody around here do anything but me?" or "No one shows any initiative around here" poison performance, team respect, and ultimately weaken the authority of the leader. And you better believe those comments get passed on, and dissension spreads like a virus. The employees think, "If he tells me that about her, I wonder what he says about me to everyone else."

Other people rarely speak unbidden in the presence of a poor leader, and will often stop speaking when a poor leader approaches. They know the poor leader has power over them, so they maintain a "bow and scrape" attitude.

The Bottom Line: Poor leaders reveal their lack of effective leadership skill with everything they say.

"The Bottom Line is that Poor Leaders don't listen."

What a Poor Leader Does

Toxic leaders are driven by ego, thrive on control, and suppress the creativity and innovation of their team.
– Brigette Hyacinth, international keynote speaker, bestselling author and thought leader

Poor Leaders:

- Are judgmental,
- Look for people who make mistakes,
- Micromanage, and
- Pull rank.

These actions are toxic. There is no way to calculate the cost of this in lost profits, increased costs, poorer quality, not to mention the cost of motivation loss for team members.

Poor Leaders:

- Don't trust their subordinates, perhaps due to a lack of confidence in their own leadership abilities. Thus, poor managers often think they have to do it all; they "do" instead of "lead;" and
- They are always too busy to listen, but when *they* feel the need to talk, it must be right now.

These kinds of actions send the message to the team that the leader feels entitled, more important, and higher in status than the workers.

Poor Leaders:

- Blame the employees for any problems. They don't view their role as solving the employee's problems. Instead, they tend to dictate problem solutions without consulting those who know the most about the work: the employees. This often leads to a sub-optimal solution.

- Do not make eye contact or call employee's names as they walk through the work area.
- Only occasionally attempt to talk with their people, but in such an insincere and narcissistic way that it's actually counterproductive.
- Employees react by sharing notes together in pairs or in larger groups about what "he" or "she" did today. They freeze up when the poor leader comes around. Open communication and transparency do not exist in these teams.

The Bottom Line: Poor leaders don't listen. They destroy morale and cost the business money in a myriad of ways including turnover, missed work, low output and poor quality, and cause passive-aggressive behavior by others.

Poor Leaders Stubbornly Resist Change

Failing organizations are usually over-managed and under-led.
—Stephen Covey, author The 7 Habits of Highly Effective People

Earlier in this chapter, I wrote that effective leaders learn. In contrast, poor leaders don't change much over the years, and they aren't much interested in learning new things. They block change and/or deny the reality of the success of change initiatives. They dismiss anything they aren't already an expert on. They often suffer from "Smartest-guy-in-the-room syndrome."

The toxic leader **pushes** teams toward success while not helping the team improve on its weaknesses. These bad leaders view themselves as "victims" who could succeed if only they got rid of their sorry crew and were allowed to hire competent staff. Often, they feel they must do everything in the business; they don't know that their role is to lead. They don't even know the meaning of the terms.

Senior managers—themselves not always poor managers—nevertheless *are* creatures of the existing culture. They are generally proud of their ability to climb the greasy pole of the engineering world up into senior management, and usually see little reason to change anything. After all, that's the system that allowed them to prosper!

They belittle concepts like trust, accountability, communication, and transparency as "Squishy stuff." Instead, they will talk about how things were in their day, and how they gutted their way through the challenges they experienced, or how they knew what to fix and didn't need risk logs and metrics. Schedules are a sort of joke to these folks.

These types of toxic managers own the moment when the moment feels good. They take ownership of positive results, but find a scapegoat when things go bad. They're always looking for their next promotion or position. Their key focus is themselves.

Poor leaders often tried to block the innovations I brought into various organizations. I often felt that long-time semiconductor senior managers didn't like "this amateur from elsewhere in the corporation coming in here and making us look bad." In fact, one VP in the semiconductor industry told me, *"You couldn't have done that [hit seven schedules in a row] around here."* Schedules in this industry are too hard to estimate accurately. *"You must have sandbagged the schedule [put in extra time for tasks]."* Well, we didn't. "Scheduling for Success" in Chapter 8 will provide more information about this.

Such an attitude might have been understandable before we were successful. But after we hit seven schedules in a row, you'd think doubters would start to come around. Somehow, that VP couldn't or wouldn't face the reality, and thus he and his teams failed to gain the advantage of new learning.

A team performs as well as it is led. If you hear senior managers say something like, "Things are so screwed up here," challenge them and ask, "Who created this culture?" Pause. Then say, "*You* did!"

The Bottom Line: Poor leaders focus on themselves, and—lacking imagination and empathy—maintain the status quo.

Why Poor Leaders are So Bad

You can't deny *bad people management* is big business. Remember the quotes in the prologue that 60-70% of technical projects fail. Think of all the money spent on processes that have been invented to try to change the bad results.

Clearly, people management gets worse the higher one gets up the organization. Managers in high tech companies are notorious after all—well lampooned by Dilbert and so forth—for being horrible people managers.

Could it be deliberate? Nah. Most poor managers have no choice but to improvise their way to success. That is, they must intuit how to advance, how to proceed every day. They try this and that, but with little overall planning. Mostly, bad management is born in or beat in along the way.

They look around, study senior managers, watching what they do, not so much what they say. They attend training classes but quickly get the message that this stuff may be OK to assuage the employees, but geez, Louise, don't believe that BS!

They are told repeatedly in these classes how to improve their approach, although I always got the feeling that most senior managers didn't truly care. Bad managers absorb no real training in a process that actually might help them be better leaders.

Except for Lisa Su of AMD and Jensen Huang of Nvidia, I bet you can't name a really good technical team leader. Elon Musk? Don't even go there.

Do the CEOs you're aware of look so smart and capable? Probably not, from discussions I've had with tech workers.

"As the leader, the culture you create with your teams is your responsibility."

PART TWO

Now that we've covered what effective leadership is and isn't, and how failure can inspire future success, let's move on to culture. As the leader, the culture you create with your teams is your responsibility. Culture is the set of informal standard behaviors and actions that are followed within the team. You have to understand that and consciously craft an effective culture, one well matched to the team you are leading.

This section will cover my foundational values and the key phrases that define the lasting culture I want to create.

The values and phrases that define your culture might be similar to mine or quite a bit different. That is as it should be. In order to be effective, they need to be yours, consciously crafted after thought and research. And with experience that includes continuous learning.

Culture eats strategy for breakfast.
—Peter Drucker, Austrian American Management Consultant
Educator, and Author

CHAPTER THREE

The Desired Culture

The very essence of leadership is that you have to have a vision. It's got to be a vision you articulate clearly and forcefully on every occasion. You can't blow an uncertain trumpet.
—Theodore Hesburgh, past President University of Notre Dame

Leadership is the capacity to translate a vision into reality.
—Warren Bennis, consultant, and author

My vision, that is, my desired *Team Culture* is below. I work constantly to implement it and use it to help my teams be effective.

A team that:

- Consists of individual contributors, management, and senior management committed to the goal of delivering the product to the customer **when we say we will.**
- As much as possible, makes team decisions (good ones!).
- Owns its schedule piece at the lowest possible level (creates/understands/updates).
- Uses valuable metrics to help manage its tasks.
- Documents "risks" at the working level and creates mitigation plans; and

To enable this, the Team Leader must have a set of standards, an ethos, if you will, bought into by the team. The standards underlie everything that goes on within the teams. I share my preferred ethos for effective leadership in the next section.

Ethos for Effective Leadership

There are three essentials to leadership: humility, clarity, and courage.
—Chan Master Fuchan Yuan, master of Chan (Zen) Buddhism

My essentials to leadership are different from those of Master Yuan, and your leadership essentials may be different from mine. That's the whole point: my ethos; your ethos.

Ethos is defined by Merriam-Webster as the *distinctive character, sentiment, moral nature or guiding beliefs of a person, group, or institution.* The guiding beliefs in my team culture are *Integrity, Transparency, Accountability, Communication*, and *Trust*, the last two only coming after the others are in place.

Find *your* ethos. Don't simply ape the approach of others. Here are a few words on each of my guiding beliefs.

Integrity

The supreme quality for leadership is unquestionably integrity.
—Dwight D. Eisenhower. 34th President of the United States

(Integrity is) Intellectual honesty. The ability to see things the way they are, and not as the observer would like them to be seen.
—Peter Drucker. management consultant, educator, author, key contributor foundations of modern management

Integrity comes from the Latin word *"Integritas"*, which means *"wholeness,"* so appropriate in a team leadership setting.

The Random House Dictionary definition is *"Adherence to moral and ethical principles."* In my team culture integrity is being honest and having the right set of assumptions internalized by all on how the team will conduct itself.

Furthermore, integrity in our team culture means we:

- Meet the corporation's goals (Although we may negotiate them!)
- Create a positive work environment.
- Find and fix the problems that need fixing.
- Have a Continuous Improvement mindset.

- Are consistent. The leader who is inconsistent, that is, happy one moment and enraged in the next for no apparent reason, will destroy any team; and
- Be direct, specific, and non-punishing to each other in all forms of communication.

I never had a team reject this approach.

Accountability

Responsibility equals accountability, accountability equals ownership, and a sense of ownership is the most powerful thing a team or organization can have.
—Pat Summit, coach, 8 NCAA championships, Olympic gold medal

Holding yourself and the team members to what each of you say you are going to do is being Accountable. That is, everyone does their job and expects others on the team to do the same. Not just the workers, but also you, especially you, as their leader

"Help solve problems. It is that simple."

An Accountable Senior Manager

I was brought into a semiconductor design center to help them learn how to meet schedules and commitments. "Scheduling for Success" in Chapter 8 describes that situation, but this story focuses on the accountability undertaken voluntarily by the VP of the center.

When Brian, the engineering design manager, and I explained our approach to the VP, he immediately asked what he could do to help. I said, *"You can tell the entire design team in an all-hands meeting that you support us. That Brian and I are responsible for fixing their problems and if we can't, we'll bring them to you, and you'll fix them."*

And he did exactly that. As Brian mentioned in an article I later wrote, *"after that it was clear to everyone that our management was totally committed and supportive of what we were doing from the start, which made it a lot easier to drive change throughout the organization."*

Our VP held himself accountable, and did his part to help us solve problems. It *is* that simple.

"Transparency is the filter applied to information communicated within the team."

No One Ever Asked Us

This is my favorite example of finding out a team's problems and then fixing them. I once went into a factory that primarily used manual soldering. It was for a space application and great dexterity was required. Almost all of the sixty assemblers on the team were women.

They had been beaten down by the world.

The factory had previously been managed in a controlling way that treated the employees like commodities, not as thinking human beings who had things to contribute, something I came in determined to change.

I started by hosting small team meetings, each with maybe eight to ten people. I would start the meetings by saying, "I want to know what needs fixing around here." At first, no one would say a word. They had been trained. Mum's the word!

I would then say, *"We'll fix what's wrong. Just tell us what the problems are."*

After a while I got them to talk. It was a slow process. When they finally opened up, I wrote down every issue they raised. I made sure they saw me do so.

Some of the problems weren't huge, or sometimes seemingly all that important, but I was working a bigger issue, which was the establishment of my personal accountability and building trust with the team.

The action item list was available for everyone to see, showing all raised issues. At the top of the document was a small box which listed "X" items resolved, "Y" items still open.

I emailed the list to the team's management group, and held them and myself accountable for fixing the team's issues. Some personnel changes for those who couldn't adapt occurred within the team's management.

We had frequent, perhaps not weekly meetings, where all the items were addressed. Within a year and a half, we stopped that process, with 900 issues raised, and over 800 resolved. The unresolved issues were no longer pertinent.

The product's quality improved, as did profits, customer satisfaction, and on-time shipments. And, of course, esprit de corps.

Trying to understand, a senior manager asked wonderingly at an all-hands meeting, *"Why weren't these issues fixed before now?"*

One of the women summed it all up, with much head nodding as she spoke. *"No one ever asked us before."*

Transparency

Transparency isn't easy. It requires courage and patience on the part of the leaders and the followers alike.
—Warren Bennis, consultant, and author

Transparency is the filter applied to information communicated within the team. Its effect is the opposite of opaque, which is what many management styles are. Teams need to be told the things that affect their success. Encourage/teach/coach your teams to be transparent.

Transparency in my culture means I take the time to tell the team what we're doing, and what is going on that affects them and why. If done honestly, your team members will believe what you say is in their best interests, not yours alone, and certainly not in management's. This is much more effective if you have first established a culture of integrity. All five of these qualities work hand in hand.

Where's the Venerable Victor

Here's a story that illustrates the lengths people have to go to combat non-transparent cultures.

One corporation I worked for went into a long decline, reducing headcount seemingly every eighteen months or so. I avoided the layoffs, but eventually left the organization for what would turn out to be much greener pastures.

No one in the organization trusted senior management's decision-making, and certainly not what management said. The general consensus was that anyone might be on the lay-off list. And, sure enough, somehow our best test technician, a guy we'll Victor—who frequently and loudly would announce his value to the team—got his name on the layoff list. He was right about his value to the organization, but the regime favored those who didn't rock the boat.

One day Victor was told *"someone was looking for him"* and he quickly disappeared into the huge test chamber area. No one in management could find him. Maybe they didn't really try, I'm not sure.

All I know is that Victor was never laid off.

After a few days management announced the layoff was over, and Victor resurfaced. He continued to work there for many more years. Sounds like fiction, but it happened.

Trust

Trust starts with truth and ends with truth.
—Santosh Kalwar, in his book Quote Me Everyday

Trust takes years to build, seconds to break, and forever to repair.
–Dhar Mann

The definition of trust in my culture is that we believe completely that we will tell each other the truth in areas where it impacts our team's success, no matter how painful it might be. Furthermore, **we trust each other and believe we will be trusted.**

Take a look at this insert from Frances Hesselbein's wonderful book, *Hesselbein on Leadership*. She gets it just right.

Trust Destroying Behaviors	**Trust Building Behaviors**
▪ Act inconsistently in what they do or say	▪ Maintain integrity
▪ Seek personal gain above shared	▪ Openly communicate vision and values
▪ Withhold information	▪ Show respect as equal partners
▪ Lie or tell half truths	▪ Focus on shared goals not personal agendas
▪ Be closed-minded	▪ Do the right regardless of personal risk
▪ Be disrespectful to employees	▪ Listen with an open mind
▪ Withhold support	▪ Demonstrate caring/compassion
▪ Break promises/confidences	▪ Maintain confidences

How to Gain Trust

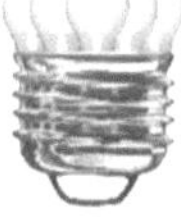

If there's absolutely one thing necessary to get anything done with humans, it is trust. Most people want to be understood, and few people have ever taken the time to try to understand them.

To get teams to trust you, show them that you can understand things from *their* point of view.

That is, use **empathy**. Understanding their viewpoint is often enough to open them up. What *you* think doesn't matter, so long as you understand what they are saying and help solve their problems.

I was often the "difficult project" troubleshooter brought in when nothing else worked. Here's the approach I used **to quickly develop trust with new teams**:

- I took some time to **get the lay of the land** before I tried to tell anybody what I wanted to change. Among other things, this allowed me to identify the most influential team members*.
- Generally, they were people the other designers worked for, but some of them were individual contributors such as the key architect or the overall project leader.
- I would then **meet one-on-one** with the key team leaders, introduce myself and share a little bit about myself. These conversations would often be stilted at first. I'd tell them I was there to help the team successfully meet whatever challenge they had been given. Of course, I quickly came to expect glances that indicated, *"Yeah, yeah, yeah, I've heard this all before."*
- At that point I would ask, ***"What's wrong around here that needs to be fixed*** *in order to help this team be successful?"*
- I would then say, and this is the key point: *"Look,* ***how about you trust me, and I'll trust you*** *to tell the honest truth in this conversation. You tell me whatever you tell me, and I'll get it fixed if I can;*

**As well as the grumblers and nay-sayers.

and, if not, I will go find the person who can. If it is just something that you'd like to tell me to help me understand, I can keep a secret." It almost always worked.

This works for one simple reason. People want to be understood. They open up, and they talk. They have so much they wish they could say, it's just that no one ever asked! Done right, they will talk your ear off.

What they would tell me I would listen to. I would take notes and then piece together what everyone told me to create a big picture of the situation.

This worked with diverse sets of people:

- The mostly male, highly individualistic engineering and design teams at two major semiconductor companies.
- A small startup where the management was quite unusual and non-empathetic.
- Teams of very dexterous, highly skilled mostly female, hand-soldering of complex electronics. I took 900 action items from one such group, and implemented a process that got them fixed.
- A team composed exclusively of young women who were millennials, and, in case you haven't worked it out, I'm not a millennial; and
- A diverse multicultural insurance office team.

Helping People Leave with Dignity

Trust is built when someone is vulnerable and not taken advantage of
–Bob Vanoreck, CEO of Sensormatic

Here is a story that gets at why employees so often these days don't trust management.

I've been scoffed at many times over the years for pushing for trust and the other four qualities in my ethos. People would say, *"It sounds fine in principal, but how do you handle sensitive issues, like layoffs or Performance Improvement Plans(PIP) ?"*

In regard to Performance Improvement Plans, I know they are often used as a way to get rid of people and are an art form in many companies. Using my values as guiding lights, I looked at it differently.

If I had to reduce headcount, then how could I do it without destroying the confidence of the PIP-ee?

I was once forced to put 1 of my 5 employees on a PIP. Reduction percentages get spread around the support organizations, in this case 20%, as you can see. Instead of grinding the employee down with the cynical PIP process such that she just quit, I worked with her to find a better match for her talents and interests. She left the company voluntarily and in a more positive frame of mind.

She got a job as an event organizer for cycling and other racing events in the Austin area, where those types of events are very popular. She has since moved on to other work that excites her. Good for her and the company met its goals.

"Trust begets Communication."

Just Communicate

The art of communication is the language of leadership.
—James Humes, author, and former presidential speechwriter

Sounds so simple

Trust begets Communication. By that I mean true, open, free-flowing communication where team members can say what needs to be said to help the team succeed, in a direct, specific, and non-punishing way.

- **Direct** means saying *exactly* what you mean.
- **Specific** means providing the right amount of detail.
- **Non-punishing** means no negative tones, no sarcasm, or diminishing of other people.

An example would be: *"the XYZ layout machine we bought last year doesn't do what we were promised and this is costing us time on the schedule. If it isn't fixed by X date, our schedule will slip."*

People talk openly with each other about issues and how to fix them. On an engineering team—people who basically don't much like to interact with the outside world—there is nothing more important to you as their leader than a culture of efficient communication.

However, the need for engineers to communicate well isn't always obvious to some people. A mechanical engineering neighbor my freshman year in college complained often about having to take an English Lit class. *"I'm going to be an engineer,"* I'd hear him bellow through the wall. *"Why do I need English classes?"*

"To discuss ideas clearly? Create plans? Convince others?" I'd ask myself.

On another occasion, a senior technical manager at a small defense contractor, upon hearing I had written a book, scornfully said, *"What good is a book?"* Taking a cue from Mark Twain's quote, *"Never argue with a fool, onlookers may not be able to tell the difference,"* I just looked at him unbelievingly and said nothing.

In this way problems are not hidden, but are brought up and discussed. Metrics, schedules, and risks (see Chapter 8) become effective tools. The problems are communicated to management, and their support is given pro-actively. No games, finger pointing, or rope-a-dope.

Why is Culture Change So Hard

From the start and throughout my career, with only a couple of exceptions, I was basically a team trouble shooter, trying to change the culture and move teams to success. Being a change agent means you threaten the status quo. Senior managers are creatures of the existing culture, as I've mentioned. There are exceptions, but they usually see little reason to change anything.

I found it easier to make culture change in an organization that had to change (i.e., improve to meet some delivery or profit goal) rather than a complacent industry leader. There were people in both types of organization who wanted things to get better, of course.

A top State Farm agent I worked with for a while was that person in business who was very successful (top 10% nationally consistently) and who wanted to make his business even better. State Farm agents as a rule, I think you would agree, generally do pretty well, so top 10% in that group is pretty good!

Here is where the complacency factor comes in. He was the only one of approximately 100 agents at a regional agent meeting who decided to work with me as their coach. He said, *"Most of these other agents are older and view their State Farm agencies as annuities, steady cash flow that they don't want to affect. Why change anything, they think?"* That is a good summary as to why culture change is so hard.

That covers the essential concepts of my desired culture: Integrity, Transparency, Accountability, Communication, and Trust. Now I want to move on to key phrases I've used frequently over the years to help team members anchor those concepts into their day-to-day work.

"Key phrases that encapsulate certain concepts can help you better define the lasting culture you want to create."

CHAPTER FOUR

Key Phrases in My Culture

A leader is best when people barely know he exists. When his work is done, his aim fulfilled, they will say: we did it ourselves.
—Lao Tzu, author of Tao Te Ching

The growth and development of people is the highest calling of leadership.
—Harvey S. Firestone, chairman of the board of the Firestone Tire and Rubber Company

The greatest gift of leadership is a boss who wants you to be successful.
—Jon Taffer, TV star of Bar Rescue

Key phrases that encapsulate certain concepts can help you better define the lasting culture you want to create. They show people what you stand for. Over my thirty-five plus year career I developed several such phrases, used so often and so apt, as to become a shorthand way to share my key actions as a leader. They follow.

"Yes, there are stars on every team, and there are many solid contributors."

Not A Rock Star

I resist the tendency in our culture to emphasize "the rock star." Everyone can contribute and we will have a much more successful organization if everyone does their best and is continuously trying to get better.

During an interview that went well a few years ago, one of the hiring managers said to me, *"Wow, you're a rock star."*

I looked him in the eye and said, *"Nope. That is exactly what I am not. I have my role. No better, no worse than anyone else."*

Yes, there are stars on every team, and there are many solid contributors. And a few, be they inexperienced, slower on the uptake, or less motivated, would bring up the rear in a top to bottom listing. But as leaders we should not be trying to make everyone into rock stars, just like we shouldn't try to hire only unicorns.

Rather, we are trying to get to yes on three questions:

- Is everybody doing a useful role?
- Is there a culture of continuous improvement?
- Is the team on a path to meet its goals?

If the answer to all three questions is yes, then you have a high-performing team. The team's output will be top notch. Schedules will be met, and quality and throughput will improve. Profits will almost certainly go up.

This is a huge deal in tech, where being first to market can often mean billions of dollars in extra revenue. Burn-out will be lower. Learning will occur. Promotions will ensue.

The outcome I seek couldn't be expressed better than by Ajay C. (Appendix B, "What Others Are Saying About Doug"): *"Doug taught us to listen to each other, to trust one another. Everyone has the ability to be great. Doug is able to bring out that greatness in those around him."*

But not a rock star!

"Hitting schedules, managing risks, using metrics, and transparent team discussion is how to show you're hard on the issues."

Hard on Issues | Soft on People

As a leader first, and a manager second, one of your most important roles as a project management professional is to cultivate and build your team's confidence.
—Ervin (Earl) Cobb, CEO and author of The Official Leadership Checklist and Diary for Project Management Professionals

Another comment I received was *"He (Doug) gets very individualistic engineers to work together by listening to their concerns but being firm about what the organization needs. I was amazed."*

That statement summarizes what being "hard on issues; soft on people" means. Many managers (poor or toxic ones) seem to think the opposite, that they have to be hard on the people to get results.

Creative people like engineers and developers hate being told what to do, and have an imperative to understand the value of what we are doing before we will truly commit.

Otherwise, we may engage in passive (or not so passive) behaviors that can render the leader's efforts totally ineffective. Being too tough with us will do it every time. Reasoning with people from where they sit is the key to being "soft on people."

Hitting schedules, managing risks, using metrics, and transparent team discussion is how to show you're hard on the issues. And, to get buy-in you must explain to the team *from their viewpoint* what the organization needs, and how they can work more effectively while not doing extra stuff they see no value in.

"Being successful requires at least some metrics and score keeping in any business or technical enterprise."

It's Not Extra Work, it is the Work

Being successful requires at least some metrics and score keeping in any business or technical enterprise.

As Brian B., a Project Engineering Manager, said, *"It would be an understatement to say that the team was skeptical of—in their words—having to do 'extra' work, but Doug partnered with the team and myself quite successfully to convince them that acting with a PM (Project Management) mindset was not extra work, it simply was the work."*

That means:

- A schedule the team have strong input into and approval of. Yes, you can question the assumptions and estimates and should push back on things that don't make sense to you. It's a collaborative effort. If treated properly teams won't pad the schedule. Try it!
- Keeping track of metrics that help the team see how they are doing.
- An accurate risk log or top ten risk list that identifies, tracks, and mitigates the major risks to the project.
- A team that appreciates what the organization truly needs from them, and that you as leader are *not* doing things to only help senior management look good or play politics.

Doing the items on the above list will pay the organization back several fold.

"To be successful as the team expert on leadership you must get actionable feedback from those affected."

Control Your Own Agenda

One secret of leadership is that the mind of a leader never turns off. Leaders, even when they are sightseers or spectators, are active; not passive observers.
—James Hume, author, and presidential speech writer

I'm a people watcher. I do so automatically, trying to understand the emotions and general state of mind of those around me. I've observed happy, sad, and all variations in between. My take away is that happiness at work is strongly influenced by whether a person is in control of their own daily agenda.

To be successful as the team expert on leadership you must get actionable feedback from those affected. I do this by enabling the team to control their own day-to-day agendas, and to have a chance to comment on how their project will be managed.

As David Graeber says in his book *Bullshit Jobs* it was Dostoyevsky who developed the theory (In his book *Notes from the House of the Dead*) that the worst torture one could possibly devise would be to force someone to endlessly perform a pointless task. You can focus teams on the organization's overall needs and help them schedule their tasks, and hold them accountable, but **you do not control them.**

Many potential leaders down in the trenches are rendered ineffective by those in senior management and elsewhere who have agendas that are different from the team's organizational goal. You must control your own agenda to keep these people from distracting and manipulating you.

You also have to be aware of the bully games (See Chapter 6, "Games Management Plays") that management or marketing often play, and you have to know how to counter them. Your agenda cannot include signing the team up for something the team doesn't think possible. Remember, engineering or development isn't marketing. You are not committed to what marketing or management say or what they've agreed to, only to what you and the team sign up for.

Of course, you can carefully threaten to move on (See "Kill Me Now," in Chapter 7). After all, you certainly don't want to go through the pain of an impossible mission, and then fail, only to then get fired or be disgraced. Right?

Later stories such as "No One Else in the Hospital" and "Double Date Management" emphasize what happens when the team has little ability to control its own agenda. Spend maximum effort on enabling yourself and your teams to control their own agendas.

Why I Come to Work Each Day

A leader is not an administrator who loves to run others, but someone who carries water for his people so that they can get on with their jobs.
—Robert Townsend, best-selling author, and executive

Like Robert Townsend writes above, **my prime task** is to make sure my teams get the help and support they need to be successful. That's what gets me up in the morning.

It can be a surprise how much effort this can take, but also surprising how much extra time you have when you are not playing politics or reacting to toxic managers' attempts to mess with you.

This starts with sharing the organization's goals to the team. The team's commitment to these goals is key. Management's goals can and should be questioned, and a mutually agreed to solution committed to.

If senior management can't clearly explain the need for an organizational goal, then something is wrong.

Blending the needs, thoughts, skills, and motivation of the team with the organization's business goals is the crux of the whole matter. The success I've had comes from doing exactly that.

To do this yourself you must:

- **Be strong** within yourself and how you present yourself to others. That means believe in yourself, be positive when others ask questions, defend yourself calmly and confidently especially when the questions are pointed, nasty, or negative. Never lose your temper or strike out verbally, unless you do it for a specific strategic reason and are under complete control. People must believe you're strong in order to believe you can do the whole job.
- **Listen** and incorporate what you hear into your approach. The wisdom needed here is to know how to process what you're hearing, sometimes on the fly. Learn to be quicker on your feet

by identifying and staying focused on the main point and getting the entire content of what the other person is trying to say.

- **Be organized**. Your agenda must be explainable and defendable against standard push back.
- **Present solid evidence on where your approach has worked**. If this is your first time, quote whomever you model your approach after. Heck, quote John C. Maxwell, Coach K, Peter Drucker, or any other successful outside expert. Many successful leaders are quoted in this book. Perhaps they or others you find may speak to you.

Well and Truly Listen

Listen with the will to learn.
-Unarine Ramaru, South African author, hip-hop scholar, and activist

"Management by Walking Around (MBWA)" is a widely used but often misunderstood and disliked technique. People characterize it in different ways, but they all generally mean:

- Be seen by your people,
- In their work environment,
- While you are friendly and approachable.

The overall concept is correct as far as it goes, but in practicing MBWA, managers sometimes get caught up in the idea that their time is more valuable than the worker's time, and think to themselves "I'll bother with them when it is convenient for *me*."

There are several potential problems with MBWA:

- If you haven't established trust with the team, they may view your effort as wasting their time. If you want an efficient team your team's time is not your time to waste. Also, trust is a key goal, and you should always be actively listening, whether it's in meetings, in one-on-ones, or in MBWA type situations.
- Without the proper attitude, which is that you are there to help them solve their problems, you can and will make things worse.
- When doing MBWA you might not appear friendly and approachable. Obviously, this won't help. Used well, listening becomes your normal state in people's minds, and you get the benefit of the doubt and seem friendly and approachable.
- Without a connection to what the team is likely dealing with, the time and day you "walk around" can really upset the team. Clueless management, right? Obviously, no MBWA on Monday mornings, and probably not Friday afternoons. Don't

pressurize them before the weekend. Sometimes Friday mornings can work, because people feel good on Fridays. Don't go out there if they are working on some deadline.

When you're trying this approach: walk up, catch the emotional tone, and seek to find out if this is the right time to ask questions. If it's not the right time, be particularly brief, say I'll come back, or just smile and make a mental note to return later.

If it is the right time, let them tell you things. Just listen. You must be natural—not intrusive—and tuned in to the team, as well as eager to be helpful.

You need to listen to the team's needs with feeling: that is, listen for what they mean but aren't saying. You need to convey how much you care when they tell you what is wrong, then put great energy into fixing the problems in a way that helps them.

This is leading in a way that serves the team's interests. It does not mean you are a pushover when it comes to milestones, shipments, schedules, metrics and so forth. Far from it. A big part of your job is holding yourself AND your team accountable to what you and the team has signed up for.

Remember:

- You need to make comfortable eye contact and ask them to tell their issue to you.
- After they dump their buffer (indicated by a pause in a way that tells you they are ready for a response) you then mirror back to them what you heard.
- If they correct what you say, repeat their correction word for word, then pause, waiting for them to affirm you. Repeat the above patiently until they have no more issues.
- The entire time you act as if you have been given a gift, a way to make things better!
- Thank them and tell them you will fix the problem or find out who can.
- Take a due date and action to get back to them.
- It's all about building trust and communicating in a useful way.

- A follow up email documenting the issue, needed action, and due date is also wise. Sometimes those things go into team meeting or quality circle team meeting minutes. That's fine.

If you aren't comfortable with the idea yet, practice with a spouse, significant other, or trusted friend. The biggest things you need are sincerity and empathy. The rest is a process that can be developed with practice.

"An ex-boss of mine moved to New Mexico and found a great job and place to raise his family. Many years later we got together for an interview for my first book."

Does That Weigh Enough

Simplicity is the ultimate sophistication.
— Leonardo da Vinci, inventor, painter, scientist

Simple does not mean easy.
—John Scalzi, Hugo award winning author

An ex-boss of mine moved to New Mexico and found a great job and place to raise his family. Many years later we got together for an interview for my first book.

We had struggled at first when I worked for him. I absolutely hate being told what to do in the tone of voice that says, *"I'm the boss and you should do as I say."* Advice, when asked for or when needed, works best with me.

He and I eventually talked it out, learned from each other, and I ultimately succeeded in his organization.

He had a PhD and had been an Air Force Colonel, so he was a bit rigid. But when we met for the book interview, it really struck me how much happier he was. The conversation was open and free flowing and much better than I had anticipated.

His job at that time was with a government entity, and he was responsible for the *"project plan,"* a required document. In the world of government contracting these are long, repetitive, and boring dirges (but contractually binding) that are generally a CYA kind of thing used to dot the "I's" and cross the "T's." Even so, words can be vague and mean different things to different people. Both sides like that "flexibility."

However, my ex-boss was quite precise and thus liked finding better ways to do required things. Therefore, his plan consisted entirely of red-yellow-green stoplight charts, with percentage bands that triggered various actions. It was innovative and I liked it.

But when he presented the document to his government customer, who was used to much larger documents, they asked, *"Is it thick enough?"* Ultimately, they allowed him to use it, and it worked out well.

Seeing a place for common ground, I related to him the first conversation I had with an unsuccessful exiting predecessor in a job where my mission was to change the culture. I'd asked that person to show me the schedule for the project. *"Oh,"* the fellow had said. *"It's over here in the corner."* He brought out a huge multi-page document, so dusty that it obviously hadn't been opened often.

Knowing what he was likely to say I asked, *"How much do you and the team use it?"*

"They don't use it all," he said. My opinion confirmed, I nodded. He continued, *"I work on it on my computer all the time trying to keep it updated. It's about all I have time to do."* Instant red flag for a likely failure mode.

I took a different tack.

I helped the team generate their own schedule. The initial response of senior managers, *"Is this detailed enough?"* was essentially the same as that experienced by my ex-boss, who laughed ruefully upon hearing my story.

I spent about two hours a week updating (freeing much time for other activities) our much simpler schedule, and it was ultimately viewed as quite useful by the team and senior management.

In both cases, the senior managers/customers valued huge amounts of data, much of it useless, rather than a useful focused approach that hit the key issues and drove the needed actions.

The best way to deal with this is to build trust with them. Often this is quite difficult, depending on built-in biases with some of them. In Chapters 6 and 7, I go into this aspect a bit more.

Over Perform, Period

Over Perform/Under Commit is what we are often told is the way to success. People intuitively get the words. So why does the opposite so often happen?

This has to do with:

- Overly aggressive commitments from marketing or management.
- A two-schedule mindset wherein ineffective senior leadership takes extra time out of the team's schedule (without reducing the required work) and uses it as a buffer, pressurizing and demoralizing the team.
- Time wasting by ineffective senior management on items like tiger team meetings (where several expensive people get together to tell you how to fix your project, see Chapter 6), the chasing of one's tail with non-value actions given at monthly reviews, too many nonsensical metrics, and the like.

Here's how to over perform every time. More detail about how to do this is in Chapter 8.

- **Schedules.** I want schedules to have estimated times as if an *average* engineer or developer does the work. One of the recurrent questions I am asked is: "Are the estimates for a senior engineer or for a junior engineer?" Answer: If all tasks are estimated as average, then we can assume—given no information to the contrary—that some will be done by senior engineers and some by junior ones, thus averaging out. Thus, we want to use the average estimate.
- **Metrics and Risks.** Show the entire list of metrics and risks at reviews as management usually insists, but always highlight the five or so key metrics and the few key risks that you and the team have agreed to manage by. As V.F. Ridgeway said, *"What gets measured gets managed—even when it is pointless to measure and*

manage it, and even if it harms the purpose of the organization to do so." If taken to the illogical extreme, metrics and risks can be twisted to say whatever the speaker wants them to say. I've seen 30 metrics required on one project *("Unmangling the Metrics"* in Chapter 8 relates that), and long lists of risks for project reviews. This often results (deliberately or otherwise) in every department being able to point to a successful metric or risk abatement from their viewpoint and to use a different one to blame someone else.

- **Accountability**. Keep good team meeting minutes, they are a great way to hold people accountable later in the heat of the moment. I've often called BS on someone's statement by referring back to the minutes. Some people want the agreements on scope of work to be fuzzy, and sometimes even they are surprised and glad we have the record. People's memories (mine included) are sometimes fallible.
- **Assumptions.** Build a culture where people speak in a direct, specific, and non-punishing way so that the confusion caused by assuming (See "Assumption Chasm" in Chapter 5) is minimized. When we don't do this team members or senior management don't trust that we are telling them the truth. This becomes a negative loop as people don't trust others if they think they're being controlled, as opposed to supported, and it escalates.

As I discuss later, sometimes senior management, who have the organizational power to control, think the best way to "help" the team succeed is to pressure them with an artificially close delivery date. This fools no one, creates a feeling of hypocrisy, and demotivates the team. No one wants to get beat up for working hard and failing to an unreasonable schedule.

Creative work, which is what tech work is, is hard enough without dealing with distracting assumptions. (See "You Can't Trust these People, You Know" in Chapter 7.)

Be aware of and have a plan to do your work based on the above list and you will have a much better chance to over perform, and to do so without working hundred-hour weeks.

Continuous Improvement

In my extended Russell family, there is a grand old matriarch, my great-grandmother Corilla, an unusual name. She was a midwife and supposedly delivered most of the children where my dad grew up.

Corilla died in 1954, but is still revered and discussed often in our extended family. However, her expression *"If you don't like my apples, don't shake my trees"* increasingly seemed wrong to me as I grew into leadership roles. Translated it means something like, *"If you don't like my ways, don't interact with me."*

Seems like good advice in a way, right? Her thinking was *"I'm not changing my ways, so let's not clash."* I have heard the *"don't shake my trees"* expression attributed to her so many times over the years. She was an area leader and people listened to her.

But not me, as this way of thinking pays no attention to and ignores continuous improvement and open communication. If you aren't seeking continuous improvement, you have a hard time growing. My view is that just accepting the status quo is not going to get problems fixed.

Instead, I think, *"There might be a better way to shake trees to get the most good apples from them."* Probably a good thing I never had a chance to suggest that to Great-Grandma Corilla! She might have shaken me!

"Be an effective leader and look for the seeming illogical logic in your team's actions, and fix the root causes."

The Seeming Illogic of Humans

We are not thinking machines. We are feeling machines that think.
—Antonio Damasio, Neuroscientist

I'm sure you have wondered why some people around you at work (and elsewhere) do things that seem so illogical. I agree, but also maintain that people, as pain avoiding animals, almost always have some reasons for the actions they take. An effective leader looks for these reasons.

Antonio Damasio, in addition to the quote above, argues in his book *Descartes' Error, Emotion, Reason, and the Human Brain*, that emotions, far from being barriers to it, are a crucial component of decision-making. Pain-avoidance is certainly an emotional response, and understanding when that is occurring can be extremely helpful.

This is why, in a culture that doesn't trust and isn't open, development teams don't bring up such basic issues as "this tool doesn't work properly," or "we need this particular skill on the team."

Me? I'd be screaming bloody murder, but the culture in those organizations sends a message like "Be quiet, don't complain, and suck it up." So, these developers just struggle along, taking the blame instead of demanding resolution. It would actually be illogical to complain in those cultures.

Why do senior managers, who would benefit enormously, not root out the problems in their organizations? After all, they have the power to do so.

Sometimes they don't know how, and sometimes, of course, the culture is so toxic that they don't really have the power. Many organizations work similarly to the way several guns can be stacked against each other so that none fall over. A dysfunctional system, in other words. In such a system there is no faith in improving things, so people just try to bull their way through. It's easier to go along, and again, this may look illogical from the outside.

Why do people back-bite, or complain about trivial things concerning their co-workers? Why do they stay in a job or an organization when they are unhappy? All of these actions seem illogical but can be dealt with by a good leader.

Be an effective leader and look for the seeming illogical logic in your team's actions, and fix the root causes!

PART THREE

This section is by far the longest of the three sections in the book. It is called "Process" because now that you understand leadership and how to create your culture, you need to know how to actually implement your leadership culture effectively into your teams.

To help you implement *your* culture, I begin with stories that highlight some of the issues that arise when leading a team. Next are chapters on the games management plays and understanding and dealing with management, followed by making effective use of the information at your disposal to help you understand how your teams are progressing.

The last chapter covers steps in implementing your culture.

"These stories come from my experience."

CHAPTER FIVE

Effectively Leading Your Teams

No man is good enough to govern another man without that other's consent.
—Abraham Lincoln, 16th President of the United States

Before you are a leader, success is all about growing yourself. When you become a leader, success is all about growing others.
—Jack Welch, past GE CEO

Failure is central to engineering. Successful engineering is all about understanding how things break or fail.
—Henry Petroski, author of many books on engineering as a discipline

Murphy Was an Optimist.
—O'Toole's Law

These stories come from my experience. Each of them covers a facet of leading your teams, and how you can sometimes be derailed by seemingly innocuous things.

"Never use team meetings to solve problems that can be solved by two people just talking together."

Don't Do's

- **Never use sarcasm** when communicating with your team (or any other time, for that matter). Sarcasm is an indirect form of communication geared to punish, to transmit criticism without taking accountability for the results. "I didn't mean anything!" is so easy to say when sarcasm is noted by the intended victim. Instead, say what you mean and use the "Direct, Specific, and Non-Punishing" trope to say it.
- As a corollary to the above statement, **be very careful about the use of humor**. A fair number of people won't think your jokes are funny. That's not to say that you shouldn't be soft on people and hard on issues. One of the best leaders I ever worked for always started a staff meeting, not with a joke, but with a brief greeting or question to each person around the table. He always included the person's name. The words, *"Hi, Doug, how are you today,"* made a huge difference on a bad day.
- **Never argue technical details** with a developer or engineer. You are a leader now. If you were once a great engineer or developer, you are not one anymore. So don't try to be "one of the gang" in areas now outside your expertise. You have enough to do trying to be an effective leader.
- **Never walk through the work area with your head down** making no eye contact. This communicates that you are too busy or too above them to notice the team. That hurts their confidence, weakens their motivation, and feeds dislike of you. All of these are negative for a high-performing team.
- **Never have a meeting where you do all the talking,** unless it is purely an informational meeting. Even then, try to save plenty of time for questions and processing of the information.
- **Never use team meetings to solve problems that can be solved by two people** just talking together.

"Watch your back and have your support nailed down."

There Will Be Blood

If you come into a new organization as a person being touted for past success in something that the current managers aren't too good at (such as what this book is about), you better watch your back. You're going to be a threat to them, unless you have overwhelming charisma.

Charismatic is not the first word I would use to describe myself. As a change agent, brought in to improve the team's performance, I would say that word would be "determined." Depending on their own viewpoints, people were all over the place in their reactions to what I was trying to do.

I place them into one of three camps:

- **People who bought into what I was doing**, either by hiring me, allowing me to do my thing inside their organizations, or on their teams. Those people never abandoned me. They are the ones who gave the comments in Appendix B.

  They understood the approach and that it could be good for them (as indeed it was). Many VP s—in the role of godfather as defined in the Dictionary of Dougisms in Appendix D—supported me because I solved some of their biggest headaches. And I generally got strong support from the working level, as their lives were positively impacted.

- **People affected in not such a great way**. These were people in mid management who were mediocre or couldn't get their brains around what we were doing.

  They could be quite defensive, or might exhibit a sneering or even blocking attitude without any concrete reason. My attitude is if you don't have a better idea, get out of the way!

- **True Resisters** were mostly from among those responsible for engineering departments or major pieces of engineering departments. Some wanted me to go away. How and under what conditions they tried to get rid of me is what the rest of this story is about.

All three times I had my legs cut out from under me, it was after a godfather left, whether voluntarily or by being politely pushed out the door. I should have seen it coming, but I was laser focused on the team and the project. I paid the price, in inconvenience if nothing else.

I knew some people felt threatened, or thought I was arrogant and over confident, or that I must be lying. Some of that was no doubt my fault. I don't suffer fools gladly (or at all, really) and I sometimes said things that were impolitic. I have an imperative to get things done and push too hard sometimes.

But a lot of it was blocking behavior on their part because they didn't want to be bothered, or didn't want someone being seen to tell them how to run their projects, even though they would have gotten most of the credit.

The first time a godfather of mine was pushed out the door, I was moved to a parallel job. The new manager said he took me because I won hard-to-win contracts (this was defense work). When I finished second on the next impossible to win contract opportunity (the first Navy UAV program), I saw the writing on the wall, and left for another part of the corporation. Outstanding results happened there on my watch, so it was all good.

Since that happened I've reconnected in a professional linked-in way with the godfather who was pushed out the door, where we support each other's ideas. He is a fine man.

In the second case, the godfather retired to his house on Lake Austin right around the time my wife took a job out of state. This godfather successfully found people in the corporation interested in hiring me there, but the move was blocked by a staff-level manager who I had disagreed with loudly and dismissively in an organizational level staff meeting. I moved on. It all worked out fine.

I saw this mentor/godfather once more, at a nice luncheon. He devoted some of the conversation to thoughts about how nice it would be to get the old gang back together.

In retrospect, he really did want to more broadly implement the improvements we were able to make, but even so quite a bit of good work was accomplished with his support. He is still in the industry and I wish him well.

The third godfather? We succeeded in his organization, but we were both out the door anyway.

Watch your back. Have your support nailed down. Do a better job than me at anticipating when and if your key sponsors (godfathers) are going to leave. It's a jungle out there in the tech world, as I'm sure you know!

"Engineers and developers live in a world where there is one working state and an infinity of non-working ones."

Getting to "Hmm: Maybe"

As a change agent, you are going to have more than just poor managers to deal with. Sometimes you'll also run across profane and recalcitrant team members.

Engineers and developers live in a world where there is one working state and an infinity of non-working ones. To survive they learn to logically trace faults and to take few risks. I've heard Civil Engineers talk about bridges that fall, Electrical Engineers talk about the cost of failed circuits or comm systems, Mechanical Engineers talk about pipes that burst with no warning. All engineers in my experience think in this risk-adverse way.

So, when someone they don't know (me or you, for example) comes into their world and wants to change the way things are done, they will have one of several reactions, sometimes extreme, as demonstrated in the following conversation.

> Me: Initial statement about my approach and how we are going to implement it.
>
> Their reaction: *"Heard that before. Not doing it."* Or: *"We've tried that before. Didn't work."*
>
> My response: *"I have examples. This has worked in defense, manufacturing, software, hardware." I'd hand them a copy of "Here's what People Say," and say, "Go talk to them without me around."*
>
> Their response: *"NO! Makes No Sense. Not doing it."*
>
> My response: *"We gotta know where we're going; management will micro manage/ direct us if we don't take control of our own fate."*
>
> Their response: *"I'm Not Going To: Eff You!"*
>
> My response: *"Some sort of management will occur. Wouldn't you like it to be...."*

Their response: *"You Can't Make Me! You're not my boss: #@!% OFF!"*

A reaction this intense and profane happened rarely, but the conversational anger occurred many times. You must stay calm and be prepared for these reactions. On occasion this is part of the job. There is a silver lining, however.

"Hmm: Maybe" is the reaction you are looking for as you patiently raise your points. There will be a cocking of the head, accompanied by a look far off into the distance.

This is great! It means you've got them thinking about it. Thinking is what engineers and developers love to do. They don't have to completely agree with everything you say (fat chance!) but once they get to "Hmm: Maybe" they may make some positive conclusions and cooperate at least a bit more.

Of course, well and truly listen (see Chapter 4), be accountable, follow the other bedrock beliefs mentioned in Chapter 3, and use the mantra "Trust and expect to be trusted." It helps if you come in with a good reputation for getting things done.

Finally, be ready with your replies to their ornery statements! They almost always come around.

Handling Resistance

Haters, Hazers, Hellions, and Henchmen

(It is) the fate of leadership to be misunderstood. It is a grave error for any leader to be oversensitive in the face of criticism.
–Nelson Mandela, 1st black president of South Africa, and activist

Generally, when you come into a new job as a change agent you run across some people who will criticize you and your agenda, or maybe just be cranky at that moment. Here's how to deal with those people.

Hazing. Light hazing can mean you are liked, and any time you come into a new job or team, there's generally going to be a period where you gradually become accepted into the team. This is tricky if you are in a leadership change-agent role, but easily done with the right personality-a solid ethos that you radiate and communicate effectively-and especially, if the team believes that they need your expertise.

For example, to the team in "You Can't Trust These People, You Know," in Chapter 7, which was a small start-up composed of quite young developers headquartered in a vibrant downtown, I was an old guy. But I won them over.

From the team interview—ten plus people around a table watching me and asking questions—all the way through my last day there, the team treated me great, never losing faith in my ability to help them meet a looming deadline for a worldwide streaming event. The hazing came from one of the more fashionable developers kidding me about the cardigan gray sweater I wore in the overly air-conditioned office.

My favorite friendly jab from him was, *"You know,"* gazing at me in my Mr. Rogers sweater, *"You pull that off."*

Laughing, I'd reply, *"What's that?"*

"The gray sweater. It works for you."

An example of less friendly hazing occurred quite early in my career. I was an electrical engineer assigned to an office composed entirely of mathematicians. Almost all of this exceedingly bright group of mathematicians were welcoming and friendly.

The not so nice hazing came from several brilliant abstract mathematicians who were deeply into things like treasure hunts and the like, with obscure and obtuse clues. I, not being a puzzle person really, declined to participate.

This reaction was anathema to these folks, and they undertook several irritating actions, including leaving clues just for me at my desk, and acting generally like I was a dull person. Reaction? *"Smile and wave, boys,"* as Skipper the Penguin from the Madagascar movies, would say.

Stay positive, keep doing what you are doing, and don't ever act angry. You might *be* angry, just don't show it. Key take away: **Don't dissipate your energy on "problems" that are ego based versus being real impediments to the team's success**.

Haters. Some people hate any kind of newly imposed structure. Haters can be identified by statements like, *"This project management stuff doesn't work." "Waste of time." "Squishy bullshit." "Non-value add,"* even before you've tried anything new.

My job, as I saw it, was to **add the minimum amount of structure needed to ensure a successful outcome for the team**. This usually meant a do-able schedule, key actionable metrics, some awareness and mitigation of risks, and simple approaches for useful team meetings and periodic management reviews.

The haters think if you're not a developer or hands-on engineer, then you must be useless, this generally having been their experience with "management." They certainly aren't wrong in being skeptical. The next two chapters cover several issues you may have with management, so I get it. After all, we technical people can be asocial or even anti-social creatures, and some of us viscerally "hate" anyone we don't respect who tries to tell us what to do.

Haters are not to be catered to. You can almost never bring them over to your viewpoint. Don't waste much time trying to do so. This is where a bedrock approach to your values comes in. Just keep doing your thing.

Hellions are the rambunctious ones who try to disrupt you because they can, just for the fun of it. Maybe they're bored. Like Loki, trickster from the Norse legends, they just act capriciously. They don't hate what you're doing, they just want to toy with you. Maybe it's amusing to them. Maybe they're just seeking attention. Who knows.

Much like hazers, hellions are to be smiled at and the behavior ignored as long as it doesn't interfere with anything useful. If the team leaders are solid with your ethos and the overall approach you take, peer pressure will push these behaviors aside. Serious business is being done, and the team leaders will do everything they can to ensure success.

Henchmen. Sometimes there are people who resist you because they are trying to curry favor with someone in the hierarchy. Maybe they work for senior managers in the affected departments who don't want it to be obvious that they haven't already done these easy and cool things you are doing, or they can't be too overt about resisting you.

These henchmen try death by a thousand small cuts. Unless they manifest major power from a senior manager, you just need to put up with it and deflect.

For example, at a monthly review these henchmen might bring up some pet metric, maybe the scheduling process, or another issue with which to give you a hard time. You've got to be prepared for this. You can bullpen the issue (see "Bullpen Items" later in this chapter), look for support from present team or senior management supporters, godfathers, or say something like, "*Yes, we've talked about that before. In this situation the team is doing this or that, and not what you are suggesting.*"

The henchman may then follow up with, "*Well, maybe it's time to readdress this issue.*"

Follow that with some variant on the statement, "*Well, maybe, if we had time. But doing so would add time or cost or risk (take your choice) and the customer/the marketplace/name of scary VP or higher person wouldn't like the result.*" That usually shuts it down for the moment. Just move on.

"You must believe one of your responsibilities is to dig out problems from the team and find a way to fix those problems."

Let Them Drain Their Buffers

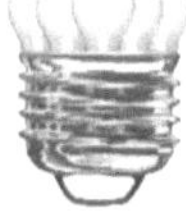

How to get your people to talk openly to you? You must let them drain their buffers. This phrase comes from the computer world, where instructions awaiting execution are often stored in caches or buffers. Unexpected instructions often back up in the queue and slow down performance.

On tech teams, there can be a tremendous amount of hidden resentment that is never expressed clearly in a way that helps solve problems. Most of the time people just complain to each other, roll their eyes when management can't see them, or develop little "secret" insider jokes about management in order to release their tension.

If you can get teams to communicate directly, specifically, and without punishing each other then you have a chance to do great things. What I'm describing is often called active listening, but I have found that phrase does not connect as well in the tech world as does "let them drain their buffers."

Essentially, you mirror back, with clarity and understanding, what is said until it is confirmed by the employee. You then pause until they indicate they're done. If they don't do so, wait longer. They will prompt you in one way or another.

What you *don't do* might sound obvious but I've found it surprising over the years how many people don't get this.

Don't act like you are doing some sort of rote thing. That is, don't say, *"It's just what we do here."* Or, *"Yeah, management makes us do this, don't worry about it."* Those are negating statements that shut down communication. You **must** convey that you truly care about what they are saying.

Don't stare into space or look down while they talk. Make solid eye contact without staring. This is certainly not the time to be the engineer or developer in the joke, *"How can you tell which engineer is not the introvert? Answer: The one looking at your feet."* Eye contact conveys how important you feel the message is.

Don't trivialize what they tell you by trying to explain the "answer" then and there. Write down their concern. And sometimes people figure something out while they're talking and they may say to you, *"Never mind." Great!*

Finally, you must believe one of your responsibilities is to dig out problems from the team and find a way to fix those problems. This is not mere record keeping. It is a way to lead your team to success.

Assumption Chasm

(AKA the color blue problem)

Misunderstandings of all types occur frequently on technical teams composed of engineers and developers, especially in the fractured cultures most organizations seem to have. Some of the most damaging misunderstandings occur in how assumptions are formed.

Different assumptions emerge based on factors like time with the company, age, what previous employer's cultures were like, and amount of experience in a particular function. An assumptions chasm emerges.

I've also on occasion called this the color blue problem. That refers to a thought experiment where you ask a collection of people in a meeting to think about the color blue. Each person, based on their assumptions, almost always thinks of a different shade of blue. Learning occurs when you point this out.

You should then emphasize that you want a culture where people speak in a direct, specific, and non-punishing way so that the destruction caused by assumptions is minimized.

And then, if you dare, share MIT professor Edgar Schein's theory: *"organizational culture is a pattern of shared basic assumptions that a group working together for a common goal has created in learning to cope with the problems of external adaptation and internal integration."* A mouthful for sure.

We want those shared assumptions to be based on integrity, transparency, accountability, communication, and trust in support of the team's overall goal.

"Much time can be wasted in team meetings solely on splitting the hairs of technical issues."

Little Endian: Sorting the Wheat from the Chaff

I've always heard "It's the Hatfield and McCoys" (usually voiced with frustration from an onlooker) defined as a heated argument over no real difference. I often used this expression when two team members, usually from different functions—maybe test and engineering—would argue vehemently from their different viewpoints.

I changed my expression of choice when I heard about the little-endian vs big-endian controversy. The first time I ran across it the word "endian" was expressed verbally, so I thought the argument was related to either Native Americans or motorcycles. True.

"Endianness" is actually about the byte address order in a computer system. Big-endian is an order in which the "big end" (the most-significant byte) is stored first. Little-endian is an order in which the "little end" (the least-significant byte) is stored first. That matters, because some computer systems read bytes from left to right while others read right to left.

Issues arise when a system using one endian format needs to communicate with a system using the other endian format. In that case, much confusion can ensue.

These terms originated with Jonathon Swift in *Gulliver's Travels.* The Lilliputians were split into those who preferred to break their eggs from the big end and those who preferred the little end. I kid you not. The intended irony of this didn't seem to translate intact into the computer world once the arguments started about "endianness." Or maybe it did, developers often have odd senses of humor.

The point is, of course, that there is no real value in doing it one way over the other way, as long as it is clear which is which. Developers will argue issues similar to this until they are spitting mad. This is because they are trained to find the right answer, and that will naturally depend on their particular perspective and the ensuing assumptions that they make.

Much time can be wasted in team meetings solely on splitting the hairs of technical issues in just this way, with nothing being decided. The best decision is the one that balances the two viewpoints being argued against what they mean to the deliverable in terms of things like cost, schedule, scope, customer satisfaction, and risk. (See "Asking the Right Questions" in Chapter 9).

In a Sentence, Please

Of course you want your team communicating with you.

But what about the small number of team members who actually *over* communicate?

You surely don't want to push them away. Whether it helps you to understand them or is a real problem within the team's assignment, they are saying something you need to know, just perhaps not succinctly.

But you don't want to be an emotional sponge either. What is an emotional sponge? Someone who is viewed by others as a person where they can dump their negative energy, to complain about something so they can feel better for some period of time.

Being an emotional sponge is exhausting. Emotional sponges are people-pleasers. They can burn out very easily trying to help others with their problems while keeping their own to themselves.

We are not psychologists, but here's something I've found over the years that works pretty well. It validates the employees. It also allows them to drain their buffers, as mentioned earlier.

I once had an employee who would rush in almost daily with the new problem of the day. I finally wrote the questions below on the white board in my cubicle. It got to the place that I would just point to the questions before she started talking.

The three questions were:

- In a sentence, what is the issue?
- In a sentence, what have you done about it, if anything?
- In a sentence, what more is needed to solve your/the customer's/someone on the team's concern? That is, what is your plan?

You ask each of these three basic intro questions, with an optional one if needed, which we will get to in a moment. Then you listen and let them talk until their buffer is drained for each question asked. You then repeat what you heard and ask, *"Do I have that right?"* Once they agree, write the statement on the white board, making mods until they agree it is correct. Then move on to the next question.

Usually even the most emotionally upset person can formulate answers to the first two questions. They often get stuck on the third question. I then ask my optional question, which is:

"What help do you need from me?"

This shows concern and often breaks the log jam in their minds. You're also not limiting their response, as you left off the phrase "in a sentence."

They came to you because they didn't know what to do. But if you spoon feed them *your* solution to *their* problem you are not helping them grow. Most people in teams have learned to not bring up issues at all, much less clearly, probably because they fear the ball will come right back to them, or lack training in clear communication. Also, shame/embarrassment often stop people from asking for help.

Following this approach helps you to put your "money where your mouth is" and to show accountability yourself. If they question whether you have the power to fix their problem, tell them you will find out who can fix it. (See "An Accountable Senior Manager" in Chapter 3).

Very rarely after all this has anyone asked me to solve their problem, even the employee mentioned earlier in this story. Generally, they just want to talk it over with someone non-judgmental. They're smart, they can think. They quite often figure it out for themselves as you talk together.

You Can't Test the Employees!

Seek to understand, then to be understood.
-Stephen Covey, author of The Seven Habits of Highly Effective People

I've always found questionnaires and assessments interesting. Early in my career, I ran across the Myers-Briggs Type Indicator (MBTI), based on Carl Jung's work. There are free evaluations on line that are good. Not quite as detailed as the full assessment you pay for, but just fine for insights or learning. This fact will play into this story shortly.

The first time I took it (it can change a bit based on life experiences and so forth) I tested as an INTJ. I for Introvert. Oh, no! A weirdo! Not true. Introverts have a rich internal world of thoughts, data, and creativity. That is where their mental energy is recharged. As Susan Cain says, in *Quiet,* "Introverts often work more slowly and deliberately. They have mighty powers of concentration." Extroverts get energy from interacting with other people. Susan Cain again: "Extroverts tend to tackle assignments quickly. Extroverts are the people who will add life to your dinner party." Both types are fine. Engineers are often introverts. Salesmen are often extroverts.

"N" for intuitive, as opposed to "S" for sensor. N-types think in less linear ways. Their thinking can jump immediately from A to Z, as opposed to S-types who must have concrete data; often believing something only if they can touch and feel it.

"T" is for thinker, as opposed to "F" for feeler. This characteristic is how data is filtered by your brain. T-types often begin sentences with, *"I think..."* F-types start with *"I feel..."* Thinkers have feelings. And feelers think just fine. Just so you know.

Finally, "J" for judger; as opposed to "P" for perceiver. Judgers make decisions. Sometimes, if they are perfectionists, they can go too far and keep asking for more and more data (See "Bring Me a Rock" in Chapter 6). Perceivers can see both sides of issues and thus often have a hard time making decisions.

I read all about Myers-Briggs, and still use several books in my work. Since I personally had learned so much from it, I gave a shortened version to all sixty of my factory employees mentioned in "No One Ever Asked Us" in Chapter 3.

They learned a lot about themselves and each other. Two examples.

First, as would happen occasionally, an employee came to my office to complain about a coworker's faults, irritating quirks and so forth. I listened noncommittally, just draining her buffer; hearing her out. She didn't ask for action. I asked her MBTI type. She told me.

About ten minutes after she left, the person she had complained about came in. He complained about her foibles. This often happened, as people were prone to watch where those they were angry with went. I asked his MBTI type.

Sure enough, they were fundamentally different. One was an N; one was the opposite S-type. One was a P; one was a J.

I got the two of them back in my office and pointed this out. I then asked each to consider if the other person's MBTI assessment on certain issues might on occasion be a strength. For example, J-types will make decisions! Perceivers can appreciate that. They looked at each other; nodded, and agreed that they hadn't looked at it like that.

Second is a story concerning a technical writer who was one of the very few F (for feelers) on the team. I made it a point to be available to talk by walking around the work area, not interfering, a smile on my face. "How are you…," that sort of thing. You get to where you can tell when someone wants to speak longer with you.

During one such walk, I ran across this woman smiling at her desk. She stopped me and said, *"You'll like to know that Myers-Briggs test really helped me understand all these technical people around here."* We had several engineers on the team, and even a few of our assemblers were T-types (the opposite of F-types).

"I thought there was something wrong with me," she continued, *"feeling all these things about work and life. And everyone around here being so grim faced."*

"Stoic and seemingly not too friendly?" I asked.

"Yes, exactly," she said. She looked intently at me. *"Thank you so much!"*

I said she was welcome. I was glad it worked out for her and went on about my business. MBTI is great for understanding diversity of thought and personality.

I was feeling pretty good until one of the engineers told her an inappropriate joke. She complained to HR and in the "investigation" she mentioned that she realized engineers, not being feelers, were less sensitive than people like her.

That odd use of language led the HR person to ask more questions. Eventually, they discovered I had given all of my employees the MBTI. I was told in no uncertain terms "You Cannot Test the Employees!"

Mea culpa. I saluted the flag, apologized, and left. I never did stop sharing assessments and learning from them, though.

"Being perfect is impossible. Excellence and continuous improvement are what we seek."

Perfectionism and Being on Teams

Being perfect is impossible. Excellence and continuous improvement are what we seek.

Perfectionism comes from anxiety. Developers often tend to perfectionism if there is no alternative structure (culture) in place. This, I believe, is because no culture equals no guidelines on how to act, and, in lieu of guidelines, engineers and developers default to perfectionism.

Characteristics of Developers

- They are individualistic.
- They've probably never been on any kind of team they liked.
- They are almost certainly introverts. This is not a bad word. (See previous story)
- They are uncertain about how to communicate or receive difficult truths. You have to proceed so carefully with this.

By the time I had worked for months with the same designers or developers, they would generally get the continuous improvement idea, and were often relieved.

They are smart and observant, and just need coaching in how to do work together constructively. Left to their own devices, designers prefer to sit in their cubicles and perfect their tasks versus talking about difficult matters that cross functional barriers.

It's just that they would just rather work alone, partly because of their nature and partly because they've had few positive experiences with teams.

A few more points:

- Designers hate to be wrong so badly they will retreat into working primarily with people they are comfortable with to the exclusion of working across boundaries.
- They hate to be criticized. Don't we all.

It is best not to criticize individuals. Developers will freeze you out from information if they think you don't approve of them.

Instead, ask key questions to get the team to work out issues; never tell an individual they are wrong. Let them challenge each other, and let the senior developers correct any technical weaknesses.

Remember: You coach individuals and lead teams.

You get to know them all and evaluate what you've got to work with. You ask yourself do I have a potentially championship winning team? OR do I have something else? Then you adjust your approach based on these things.

Here's an example. A design team at one major corporation I worked for were very good at their jobs, but they'd had no one show them how to work together, to communicate clearly, to hold each other accountable, or how to trust. And they had no one with their best interest keeping score (schedule progress). So, I concentrated on those things.

They became a championship team. Never having hit a schedule before, they went seven for seven. Bonuses were paid. People, including me and the design manager, were promoted.

Dealing with Odd Ducks

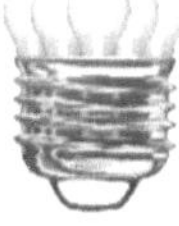

Every organization has strange people, engineering organizations perhaps more than others. Learning to deal with them is sometimes necessary.

An example might illustrate. Early in my career our engineering office had a lab just down the hall. Ostensibly this lab was supposed to do analyses to support questions we might have with the complex hardware we managed.

The fellow who ran the lab was a very smart and capable guy. He was fun and interesting to talk to. Let's call him Fred.

There was only one problem with Fred. He had an unusual way of avoiding being pinned down, of not doing what we asked when we asked. A witty technician in our office nicknamed this technique "Rope a Dope," after the boxing tactic of Muhammad Ali.

Maybe he was just lazy. Or maybe it was his way to keep himself interested. We would eventually get what we needed from him, but it was a real battle sometimes.

His tactics would vary. He might wander off in mid conversation. He might distract you with another subject. He might get vague and say *"I'll have to think about it."* Or he might say, *"I don't know if that is possible."* I still remember his grin and the gleam in his eye during these conversations.

I wish I could tell you I figured out how to motivate him, but sadly I dealt with this the whole time I was in that office. Many of my office mate engineers did their own analysis because they couldn't get him to do anything.

This guy was talented but impossible to motivate. What a waste. The things he could do with an oscilloscope were amazing.

Don't waste *your* time trying to understand folks like this. Maybe you can get them reassigned or fired. Or put on a PIP. Somehow none of those things ever happened to Fred (it *was* in the government). And don't try to find ways to appease a guy like this. You'll only frustrate yourself.

Done Done

I've noticed over the years how easy it is for people when assigning percentage work accomplished to get to 85%. And they stay stuck there seemingly forever, never able to finish.

That is why when I schedule a project, I insist on "started" and "finished" as the only two criteria for a particular task. For the schedule to then be granular enough, no task can be longer than 2 weeks. If the task is truly longer than two weeks, as estimated by team members, it must be somehow broken into realistic pieces two week or less in duration.

There is "Done" and then there is something else entirely that is called "Done Done." "Done" means "I've worked hard on this for a long time and I've made a lot of progress." As in, **"I'm done, damn it!"** They are tired of the task and feel they should be finished. This applied to homework and tests as a kid and many other things, sports practice, or presentations.

Winston Churchill captured this feeling perfectly when he said, *"Writing a book is an adventure. To begin with it is a toy and an amusement. Then it becomes a mistress, then it becomes a master, then it becomes a tyrant. The last phase is that just as you are about to be reconciled to your servitude, you kill the monster and fling him to the public."* That is the done feeling.

"Done Done" means your work is ready to ship to the customer, that it will stand up to scrutiny, and that the customer will believe they got their money's worth. This is an entirely different thing. It means no corners cut; no shortcuts taken.

How does this apply to being a good leader? Well, this is one way to not be overly optimistic early on in a project, only then, near the end, to have no progress seemingly occurring, exactly when everyone is on edge. Nervous senior managers can be quite unruly.

Think of Done Done on your next schedule!

"It is key that you evaluate your team's workplace intelligence, relative degree of cooperation, and their maturity with project management tools like schedules, risks, and metrics."

Remote Teams

So how is managing a remote team different? I had a remote team composed of people in Texas, California, and two overseas countries. The team generated excellent results.

I followed the same process as this book outlines, but modified a few things:

- **More interaction via the phone** or other devices versus face-to-face. Obvious.
- **Less process.** For example, I didn't create a detailed schedule. I just used a two-week milestone schedule, and didn't ask them to generate sub-schedules for each site's work. This was part of the approach to treat each site as its own team, with its own unique culture. I integrated the progress at the sites into the milestone schedule.
- **Metrics and Risk Logs were leaned down** to the essentials with management's prior approval.

I **didn't visit each site**, due to distance and my belief that it just wasn't necessary with these senior laden teams. I would normally visit each site at least once.

The team was composed of experienced people who didn't balk at the modified process. It is key that you evaluate your team's workplace intelligence, relative degree of cooperation, and their maturity with project management tools like schedules, risks, and metrics.

"Just understand that you can't allow distractions to the team effort."

Bullpen Item: Dealing with Distractors

Distractors, those people at meetings whose issue always seems to them more important than whatever issue the team is currently discussing, are best handled by having a "bullpen" for non-critical action items.

These distractors may be trying to thwart you, or think you are arrogant or have slighted them in some way. They may just be game players messing with you. Maybe they are zealots for a particular viewpoint. Often, this is AGILE related.

Doesn't really matter. Just understand that you can't allow distractions to the team effort. If you continue to allow it, the team's focus, trust, and respect can drop off, and you risk losing the room. You're the leader, remember.

Here's what you do:

- Simply say to the distractor, *"That is something we can talk about, for sure. Let me put it in the bullpen."*
- Go to the white board, put up "Bullpen" (Some folks prefer the team "bin list") as a title. Underline it. Write their issue below. Suggest or request the appropriate action item.
- Make sure the distractor agrees with the action item you capture. Once they do so, look them right in the eyes and ask, *"Can we go back to XYZ, the point we were discussing?"* Once they nod, go back to the point, with your discussion still proceeding.
- If they don't nod someone from the team will likely shut them down. If no one does so, say, *"We need to stay on track. How about you and I talk about this after the meeting and figure out a way forward?"* Had I done so with the guy who seemed like a distractor in "Zealot Failure" in Chapter 2, I would likely have generated a much better result. He was only trying to help.

Put the bullpen item in the meeting minutes and keep track of it. Eventually it will be clear to all whether the issue is real or can be retired.

CHAPTER SIX

Games Management Plays

You can be the most productive and most effective, but politics show up as ego, jealousy and sabotage from bosses who can't perform.
–Richie Norton, author, entrepreneur, and speaker

Ego can't sleep. It micro-manages. It disempowers. It reduces our capability. It excels in control.
–Robert K. Greenleaf, author, and founder of the modern servant leadership movement

The man who smiles when things go wrong has thought of someone to blame it on.
–Robert Bloch, author of the book and movie Psycho

This chapter gets to the heart of why only 30-40% of all tech projects succeed. I am not attacking the senior managers and VPs (See first story in Chapter 7) in these stories so much as illustrating the point that training and improvement in people management skills is badly needed.

"Senior managers often call tiger teams when the team has just about got a handle on the problems and—if left alone—could have righted the ship."

Tiger Team Meeting

Every once in a while, especially on major projects, senior managers will think they need to host what is called a tiger team meeting for projects which are "in trouble" and "can't be allowed to fail!" Attending will be the big boss in the division, a few senior managers there to watch their flanks, some high-level senior experts, and the key workers on the project. These meetings may also be called "Swat Teams," or "Special Project Units."

Probably coincidentally, senior managers often call tiger teams when the team has just about got a handle on the problems and—if left alone—could have righted the ship. Sort of like a congressional hearing on various topics of interest: no risk to the senior managers, gets them some publicity, and just might do some good.

In any case, a tiger team involves "meeting in the office of fill-in-the-blank senior manager's office sometime after normal work hours." The chosen time is often 5PM. This is the middle of the work day for many developers and engineers, but never mind, they're just expected to stop working and go to the meeting.

Developers work all hours, generally come in by 10AM (but often earlier), maybe work until 7PM, go home for dinner and work again online until midnight or past. Late at night the servers aren't as busy.

These meetings are time wasters and morale destroyers. They are for the benefit and knowledge of the senior most manager, in case he or she has to answer to someone higher. This is micromanagement at its worst. The best motivation I can assume is senior management might think the pain somehow motivates the team. (See "Pain Avoiding Animals" in Chapter 7).

Tiger Teams are all the same, so it isn't interesting to describe them in any detail. I knew many victims of them, and I saw their frustrations up close. Often "guest stars" from among the workers are also drawn in to "answer this one question," and then they shoot out of there like bats out of hell.

None of the projects that I led ever had a tiger team meeting.

I can only remember attending one tiger team meeting. On that occasion, the meetings were attended by the staff of the division, and we were each expected to answer detailed technical questions about whatever might come up in the engineering area we were to cover. The project under discussion wasn't being led by me.

If we didn't have all the details at our finger tips we were made to feel stupid (to "motivate" us?) and told to be better prepared next time. Of course, this meant we had to take a huge amount of the team's time asking detailed questions. Everyone was relieved when the product was finished and shipped to our customer.

The ending of a tiger team is often hilarious, as one-by-one all of the attendees try and eventually succeed in getting out of having to attend. Ultimately, victory is either declared or someone is replaced. Often that in itself is a sort of declaration of victory.

The award for the greatest Tiger Team caller of all time goes to the chief design engineer on "No One Else in the Hospital," in Chapter 7. I wasn't asked to attend. Thankfully.

The stress involved in working for her did send me to a stomach doctor to find out why my stomach would not empty of food. *"Clenched pyloric valve,"* the doctor said. *"Probably stress."* Uh, yeah.

Don't get put into the position of being forced to attend a Tiger Team meeting. Control your own agenda. Have a clear and easy to understand execution plan for your projects. Build trust with management, perform successfully from the start, and follow it all the way through to the end.

Bring Me A Rock

Lacking confidence concerning their decision-making ability, and on the premise that there is never enough data, some poor leaders will ask for additional data again and again. I call this "Bring Me a Rock."

Sometimes these are insecure managers who feel like you are some sort of threat. Sometimes they get a sense of control from doing this. Often, they just don't know what else to do. Often, they are hung up in analysis paralysis.

The result is that you and your team become increasingly demotivated by having to get more and more data from the people who know the minute details, wasting their time and yours. All just so you can report the details demanded by the senior manager.

These kinds of managers consider this behavior completely reasonable, so the last thing you want to do is to argue with them or say no. And being passive aggressive (sighing, disappearing) is a bad choice as well. No one likes a whiner, especially managers in tech who are under a lot of pressure. Often they are dismissive of anyone not in design engineering.

Instead, you can seek to understand their true deep-down needs, not just at the moment, but over time. When not under pressure, ask a series of questions that help you understand them. Who knows, they may answer honestly. You don't have to wait to ask them, you can start when they interview you for the job.

Sprinkle the following questions into various conversations.

- What are your biggest concerns? (Always a good first interview question)
- What has worked well/poorly in the past?
- What do you hope to accomplish here?
- How can I best help you?

After the above rapport building, the senior manager might be more prepared when you roll out the following:

- I can't do my job well if you are always changing the requirements.
- I need time to find the information you want and to prepare a proper analysis.
- I am a highly trained and experienced professional and can't do my best work (nor can my team) in this air of pressure and strain.

Designated Scapegoat

When I first became a Program Manager in the defense sector, I was assigned a contract with the scope already agreed to, and a final price already negotiated for a development effort, which are notoriously difficult to estimate. This was with a customer we couldn't afford to lose. For me it came along with being the new guy. (See "Snake Pits," Chapter 7).

This of course, was not a good position to be in, as I had to execute on the schedule and for the dollar amount without having been involved in developing the proposal or being part of the contract negotiation. Over my first few weeks, various members of the customer team hammered into my head that *"Your company always overruns. You can't do that here! We've got no more money!"* Repeat. Repeat.

Our marketing guy hammered me too. He had made the deal; one of those "hallway" chats with the customer. I got the message, all right. I was the designated scapegoat if anything went wrong.

I would have done my best job no matter what. I watched the numbers very closely as the project proceeded. In an effort to predict where we would wind up, I even took derivatives on the rate of change over time of spending by category. This is the project where I first became adamant about never letting estimators use anything other than 0/100 percent for task work accomplished.

The project was a complicated one. It required marrying together two pieces of hardware from different parts of our corporation to create a specific new product the customer wanted badly.

Two months or so before the scheduled project conclusion, I formed the strong opinion that we were going to run out of money. I went to my VP and shared the data with him. He didn't hesitate. *"You've got to tell the customer."*

I made a phone call to the customer's contract manager. A huge furor ensued. *"You promised!"* I was loudly told. I was threatened with phone calls to the CEO. It went on and on.

Finally, I was told, *"You're coming back here to explain."* A few days later I was in the ominous main building of an intimidating three letter agency in Washington, DC. Twelve or so members of the customer team awaited me in a conference room. They exuded intensity and frustration.

The only representatives from my corporation were marketing people from the other half of our corporate joint venture. They sat in the back in the room, and didn't speak to me before the meeting started. Our marketing guy, who had made the deal, did not attend. That's how this works.

With a severe frown at me, their leader nodded. Let's get started.

I stood up and said, *"We need X more dollars to complete the project. I can show you the details, and we can complete it for that amount. But if we don't have more money by Y date, we will have to stop work. It is your decision on how to proceed."*

Before I had even finished my opening statement, loud denouncing of me and my corporation began. *"We knew you'd overrun! We'll call your CEO…you promised…Your VP promised…"* I stood there and said nothing, instead waiting for them to drain their emotional energy.

I gave the same basic speech again. Same reaction. Somewhere in all that, I actually did share my detailed estimates and cost build up.

Again, a third time, never changing my speech, tone, or cadence, I delivered the same message.

I was prepared to continue to do so, no matter how many times I had to repeat the message, but, finally, they wound down. *"We'll get back to you,"* I was told menacingly.

The marketing reps from the back of the room came forward, all smiles. *"You did pretty well, Doug! Let's get lunch."* Just another day at the office for those guys.

Afterwards, I went back to my home organization and waited. Would this be the end of my "management" career before it really got started?

Nope. A few days later, I got a phone call from the customer. *"We've found the money you asked for. To the dime. You better not ask for more."*

"I won't," I said. And we didn't need more. We finished on time on a development effort for what amounted to slightly more than one-percent over the original amount.

How to deal with a hot potato discussion like this? Be polite, businesslike, non-argumentative, but firm and hold your line. Keep the same patient tone, deliver the same message, stay on point, and don't digress.

In short, don't back off from your position.

The message I stated and never wavered from was:

- We had done the best we could
- But I could see we were going to fall short
- And I had a responsibility to raise that fact early enough that they could do something about it.

Many government contractors will wait until it is too late to do anything and then raise such an issue.

Danger surrounded me if I drifted off point, and that will often be the case for you as well. Here's a couple of tactical tips:

- I never admitted any fault. That would likely have been used against me and my corporation.
- I just stuck to the facts. We had done the best we could; it was actually a good effort.
- I never said I would go talk to my VP or anyone else in our company.

That would have been viewed as weakness, a tacit admission that our corporation might split the amount with the customer or something of that order.

This is the best you can do in such a situation. Do a good job, present the facts, and stand firm with whomever is "in charge."

How did it all end? Was I fired? Lose my program manager position? Nope.

This was my second contract with the same customer. I went to my VP and asked for a new assignment.

When word of my reassignment came out, I received a call from the customer.

"Doug, is what we hear true?"

"What's that?"

"You're leaving us?"

"On to new assignments, that's right."

A pause. *"Well, gosh Doug. You were the best program manager we ever worked with at your company."*

Amazed, I laughed. *"Wow."* I paused, then said, *"I gotta' ask you this. How did you treat the bad ones?"*

He returned my laugh.

No designated scapegoat; I lived on for several years as a PM in that organization.

Declaring Victory and Moving On

Mankind is the only animal that blushes, or needs to.
—Mark Twain, author

Here's a story about how poor managers borrow tactics from politicians, not that they necessarily think of it that way. Politics is what it is. Not inherently evil, politics is just one way people get things done through other people.

In this case, toxic bad managers will try an improvement process[*] and announce that a new program, let's call it BRAIN DEAD, will be used in all organizations starting next month.

A memo will come out (I have seen many of these memos) that says something like: *We will train all of our managers (*no they won't*) in this process, and believe we will achieve X% improvement in sales/profits/customer satisfaction/employee satisfaction (pick one or more). 100% of our teams will be trained and will be using BRAIN DEAD successfully by the end of the quarter/year.*

At some point, after visible effort has been performed, BRAIN DEAD will stop, often because of complaints from senior managers to their bosses. *"Let's get back to how things were before this 'new process,'"* they'll say. *"My people are spending too much time on this stuff."*

By this time, the process will have yielded only limited success, with the basic problems remaining unfixed. Results are never as good as promised, but to save face, and to not get blamed for anything, management will declare victory to one or more of the "key" goals and move on. The mediocre truth will then be blurred with positive,

**Ask Google for a list of the top processes. I asked several times and got a slightly different list each time. I've used something like 95% of the processes on the various lists.

marginally correct statements, so that management can declare "victory" and move on.

Finding a way to "declare victory and move on" is a basic human reaction in a culture of being judged, perhaps unfairly, when you don't have the ability or skill to do what you promised or were committed to. I get it, but it would just be so much better for everyone involved if real results were obtained. But, we humans just hate to look bad.

If this happens often in your organization, you should find a new place to work. There are budding good leaders everywhere. You just have to hunt a bit for them. I did this successfully once or twice. It can be done.

Program of the Month

Shortly after the events in the previous story, management will then introduce a new process and the whole thing starts up again, as if the employees don't see what is going on.

Next month/quarter/year they will try another process. I've heard this derisively called "Program of the Month" many times.

Why do senior managers do this? Although there are a few sadists everywhere, the vast majority of terrible managers don't generally intend to make employees miserable.

They:

- Have a short attention span and without giving the new process a chance to take hold, will move on to yet another process.
- Think new processes are a quick way to maximize profits, improve customer satisfaction and quality, and ensure highly valued employees don't leave.
- Are too far away from the action to know what's really going on, and not knowing how to delegate and lead, often jump from process to process trying to find elusive improvement.
- Don't really believe in their hearts that anything is going to change when they try the next process, and they're just upholding appearances.

Well, at least it is an action. No one ever got fired for trying to improve. How often have you heard something like, *"You know how much money and time we spent on trying to improve our processes around here last year?"* So, they do get *some* points for doing something. Not too many though, since it didn't work as advertised, but still.

Of course, the employees often get blamed for not being "world-class" when improvement doesn't come. In many ways, this book is about trying to help you lead without being thrust into such a position.

My answer? After "Zealot Failure" in Chapter 2, I matched my approach to every organization I worked with. One size does not fit all, and a new process every month or quarter is not an optimal solution!

Don't play along with senior managers or anyone else who tries to introduce process after process to your teams. I remember a leader who went to management and got an exception from one of the programs of the month because it conflicted with an improvement process he'd had great success with.

Instead of all the above foolishness, the organization shouldn't try the new process on every project all at once, but should match a process to its culture, perhaps by picking one project for focus. They should then put change agents out in the organization with enough clout (overt and covert) to actually have a chance. The metrics should support the items being improved (See "Unmangling the Metrics" in Chapter 8) and, as I've stated, project and senior management should be held accountable by their bosses, instead of scapegoating those below them.

Nine Women | One Month Fallacy

Adding manpower to a late software project makes it later.
—Fred Brooks, The Mythical Man-Month

No matter how great the talent or efforts, some things just take time. You can't produce a baby in one month by getting nine women pregnant.
—Warren Buffet, investor

Poor managers will often pour additional people into a struggling project in an effort to get it back on track, but often too late to accomplish more than just muddying the waters. This is called *the "Nine-Women/One-Month Fallacy."*

This **never ever never** works in tech world. There are studies that show it doesn't work, and I would often pass around such information. In addition to the Brooks and Buffet quotes above, NASA & DOD Systems Engineering Guidelines, as well as Agile & Scrum Best Practices, mention this.

Most senior developers and engineers abhor the practice because they know they are going to have to deal with the mess. Putting many extra, even competent people (which are generally hard to get), on a project all at once creates enormous stress on those team leaders trying to coordinate the team's activities. Also, the existing people often resent or look down on the new people since they don't know the project. Also, team leaders are dealing with existing technical and people issues, as well as finding tasks the new people can be dropped into efficiently.

Getting project status from a larger team is quite often even a bigger headache. (See "Hundred-Person Wall Problem" in Chapter 7). Sometimes even additional managers have to be brought in, and this can increase the confusion exponentially.

Finally, creative work is thought-based work. Our brains can't work well in a fight-or-flight mindset, which is what a fire drill creates. Tiger Teams (see story earlier in this chapter) are often instituted at the same time, and they, as well as other senior management actions, encourage a fire-drill mindset.

Hiding the truth is endemic in low trust organizations, and the tendency to hide things gets worse in a fire-drill environment. Fault finding and finger pointing gets worse. Poor managers do this because they must be seen doing something in the face of a problem.

Sure, you say. But how did we get here? I wrote in Chapter 2 that poor managers don't trust their teams. Yet, they trust some team members, and they trust quite a few of the chief engineering people, but **the cultures they create that affect everyone are not based on trust**. And they generally didn't get where they got to by being overly trusting.

Almost all senior managers I worked with were better technical people than me. I am a member of the electrical engineering honor society, but I am not a technical genius like many of them. It's just that these folks often lack—like many people—the emotional and workplace intelligence to know how to lead teams, something they often aren't aware of.

Therefore, their first inclination is to distrust, and to only trust people based on good past experiences as well as being inclined to trust, for example, people of their own gender, people from their part of the country or university, or from their engineering specialty. Humans are wired to trust those who look and seem similar to us. The "other" seems odd.

Since they don't trust the team to tell them the truth, poor managers will often under-staff a project in the beginning. They think they are saving money; creating a buffer and/or preventing the team from over staffing. Previous projects (ultimately almost always late) had overstaffed at the end to try to catch up. Hence the nine-women/one-month fallacy. It becomes a reflexive habit.

Staffing properly all along the way is the answer to the temptation of over staffing near the end. Team Leads, if not micromanaged, will staff properly. If toxic managers would only learn to help the team leaders focus on a simple and straightforward, fact-based way of working together, much of this could be avoided.

Double Date Management

Senior managers often keep two sets of books: that is, with two different schedule commitment dates. If you live in the tech world, you probably have no problem believing this statement. If you're not in tech, you may think that statement is crazy. It is not.

Here's how it works. The top kahuna in charge (internal manager or external customer) gives a mandated date. This date doesn't need to have any bearing on reality. It's just an effort to put a line in the sand in order to drive the engineering organization, and to hopefully make competitors think they're too late to market, and thus not even try.

At the same time, management has a more realistic date in mind, but they keep this to themselves. Think I'm being cynical? Says Ajay C., now of Nvidia: *"Design managers often keep two sets of books: an internal schedule that they strive towards and an external schedule for everyone else. This tendency leads to trust issues and communication problems between groups. The problem is that most engineering managers have never had the opportunity to learn the skills necessary to become great managers."*

Everyone just salutes the flag (the early commitment) and goes about their business. They know there will be plenty of problems later to blame schedule delays on. Or the customer will change/add scope of work, and they can then weasel out of the original date based on that. Their internal estimate, whether stated or otherwise, might be many months later, and never be seen by more than a handful of trusted people.

Quite a few senior managers have told me they have to manage this way, that it is impossible to schedule a major high-tech advancement accurately. Not true!

Instead, you have to insist on a culture of transparency and honesty. Don't smirk at me, here's how it works. You tell the truth and then perform. Simple as that. One schedule is all you need. See "Scheduling for Success" in Chapter 8 for how to make a transparent schedule.

If management won't let you do so, find another job as quickly as you can. Or you can do as I write in the next chapter's story "Kill Me Now."

Denying Reality: "Problems? What Problems?"

To be a senior manager, you first have to get there.

In Tech that means you are definitely smart, highly educated, and have a take-charge persona. So, when you didn't see a problem coming, your first reaction may be to deny reality as well as deny the data. A self-preservation technique for the alpha ego.

My belief is managers deny reality because most tech organizations (indeed, most human organizations) are shame-based cultures. What happens in these shame-based cultures when the truth comes out?

- Depending on their personalities managers may attack the person who first highlights the problem.
- They will spend more time talking about why the problem isn't important than in figuring out what to do about it.
- They will try to identify the guilty; will often punish the innocent.
- They will put in over-reactive fail-safes on the next project so that this will never happen again.
- They may try foolish, knife-catching maneuvers like the Nine Women/One Month fallacy, Tiger Teams, putting the team on 12-hour shifts, or canceling vacations. That last one goes over well with the families, let me tell you.

Instead, you should work to build a trusting, transparent, accountable, and communicative culture. Much easier it is to follow a rational process of seeing potential problems coming long before they strike, and being ready to talk scope, schedule impact, customer satisfaction in a structured and organized way. This trumps denying the reality every time!

"The two-armed salute was a familiar expression to the people who worked at one of my employers."

Two-Armed Salute

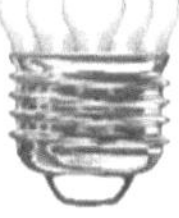

The two-armed salute—generally accompanied by a shrug and a sigh—was a familiar expression to the people who worked at one of my employers.

Some context. Organizations have different cultures around transparency, direct/specific/non-punishing communications, and accountability.

- The culture of this particular employer was generally non-transparent.
- Communications were direct, but very punishing and had an air of vagueness around them.
- Accountability was of the variety "punish those involved, but never those in charge."
- This added up to a culture with very little integrity.

Therefore, individuals, who had to survive in that organization on a day-to-day basis, came up with various ways of expressing their feelings without being seen as criticizing those in charge.

One such form of expression was the two-armed salute (see photo below), a sign of knowing and resigned acceptance to the general vagueness, lack of direction, and a certain hopelessness endemic to the organization.

If your team is characterized by those types of communication, you've got problems. It's not just a funny little "thing" people do. It's a sign of repression and will kill any team's ability to generate great results.

AI generated by author

"Like most of us, senior managers are a blend of bad and good habits."

CHAPTER SEVEN

Understanding and Dealing Effectively with Management

People ask the difference between a leader and a boss. The leader leads, and the boss drives.
—Theodore Roosevelt, 26th President of the United States

You don't manage people, you manage things. You lead people.
—Rear Admiral Grace Murray Hopper, US Navy rear admiral, mathematician, and computer scientist (Creator of COBOL)

A cowardly leader is the most dangerous of men.
—Stephen King, novelist

Management is about arranging and telling. Leadership is about nurturing and enhancing.
—Tom Peters, business management expert, and author

Like most of us, senior managers are a blend of bad and good habits. In this chapter I'll share some experiences that helped me to better understand and deal with senior management.

"Often, the tools in their toolboxes were control-oriented tools like Tiger Teams, added metrics, and extra scrutiny, all of which take creative time away from the hands-on technical people."

Spackling Over the Cracks with the VPs

In this book generally, and in the stories in this chapter, I may seem to be a bit harsh on the VPs and senior managers. I don't mean to be.

I wrote earlier that when senior managers were lower-level leaders themselves they—already not being predisposed to learning how to lead people—were rarely taught the kind of leadership skills and approaches discussed here.

Often, the tools in their toolboxes were control-oriented tools like Tiger Teams, added metrics, and extra scrutiny, all of which take creative time away from the hands-on technical people. That does not make them evil or even particularly manipulative, just humans doing what they can do to survive in a fast-paced high-pressure environment.

I will get to some positive stories about top senior managers in a bit. But first let's look at a few negative stories:

- A VP told me what we had done couldn't be done, and then wouldn't talk to anyone on the teams to check out the data presented. In essence, he denied that the process had worked.
- I had an SVP, when a corporate person called him and asked why his organization's metrics got consistently better every quarter, say to me, *"It was you, Doug."* I asked if he had told the corporate person that and he said no, he hadn't. Gee, thanks! Give a man some pub! Maybe the corporation could have used similar results?
- I had many VPs and even higher, upon interviewing me for leadership jobs in their organizations, say things like *"this is just project management that you do, why would we hire you to such and such a role?"* Well, many others would agree it was something more than "just project management." It was leadership.

Now for the more positive side:

- An IEEE VP welcomed me into her local engineering management society. We struck it off so well, she nominated me as the next leader of the chapter, thus opening me to many new opportunities.
- A senior VP supported my process early on when he could have easily not done so. He carried a lot of weight. He was a revered guy, the engineering team leader for the Motorola microprocessor chosen by Apple for the Mac and for many other applications.
- A VP responsible for a design center stood up in front of an entire team and told them we were going to do my process and he would solve any problems that we couldn't. That kind of support obviously makes a big difference.
- Another VP still promoted me even though I raised my voice at him in one of his staff meetings. Well, two different staff meetings actually. The promotion was held up quite a while, but it eventually happened.
- A VP hired me into his organization as an engineering director and did his best to help me as we coached and improved organizational performance.
- A successful State Farm agent (the VP of insurance companies) hired me early in my consulting career, and closely followed my advice.

There. Three negative and six positive comments about VPs or senior managers. Many of the people who did listen, who in fact contributed to Appendix B *"What Others Are Saying About Doug,"* have progressed in their careers nicely, partly from using my techniques. Some of them became VPs. We'll add them to the positive ledger also.

VPs and senior managers, I am not attacking you! Open your minds to these results. Imagine what they could do in your organization, and start helping your new and mid-level managers do these things. Support them.

What We Can Do When They Don't Get It

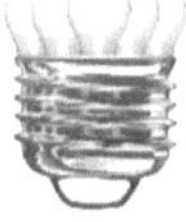

It behooves us to find ways to engage with senior managers without appearing to be suck-ups. In my experience, that was quite hard to do.

Over my thirty-five years the biggest resistors were the senior engineering managers. These were the direct line managers (not the project engineering leaders) for the teams I led, and they essentially only understood getting things done by doing the thinking (thus eliminating solutions outside their thoughts) and telling their people what to do. They didn't much like someone else *"telling their people what to do."*

They struggled to understand what I was doing and especially how I was doing it, even though I explained and briefed it many times. Essentially, I wasn't telling their people what to do. **I was leading them by showing them a successful way for them to meet their goals**. That's why they bought into what I was saying. I certainly had no direct organizational power over them.

There was always a whiff of superiority in the air around the senior managers, as in "If you were really a good engineer, you would be one of us." Funny, I always thought if only they could lead they might be like me!

As far as what we can actually *do*, my best advice is to build bridges with the senior managers who have line authority over your teams. Have monthly 1:1s with them and work to find areas of alignment.

It is also imperative that you get on the staff of the VP the senior engineering managers who have line authority report to. That VP may then serve as your godfather.

To soften the hard interface between you and the resisting senior managers, ask for your godfather's help. On at least one occasion, a SVP godfather of mine sent out a memo to his staff outlining how he wanted the organization to respond to the approach I had successfully used elsewhere in the building. This had little overt impact; who knows what impact it had behind the scenes. Don't expect SVPs to too visibly take your side. It is a battleground of ideas out there, and you've got to be able to defend yours well!

Seek other people on your godfather's staff who understand the benefits of what you're doing and ask them to talk with those resisting. Sometimes I found organizational development employees assigned to the staff who would do this.

Empathy Enmity

Empathy is being concerned about the human being, not just their output.
–Simon Sinek, author, and consultant

Empathy is the ability to see with eyes of another, listen with the ears of another, and feel with the heart of another.
–Alfred Adler, psychologist

Senior-level leaders Ervin (Earl) Cobb and Bob Carroll, both mentioned earlier, had empathy for others, and were good at leading teams. But quite often, as I've mentioned several times, other senior managers didn't know much about leading people.

It would be reasonable to ask how those folks got these senior leadership roles. The composite I would draw in the tech world is a combination of at least a Master's in Engineering with very good grades and technical knowledge, verbal dexterity, at least some charisma, and political skills.

By political skills, I don't mean they are sneaky sly devils. A few are, of course, but no more than in the population at large. Political skill is knowing which way the wind blows, reading the room correctly when you walk in, thinking ahead on what the consequences for various actions might be, and building alliances.

These of course are all good skills to have in general. In fact, these skills are very useful for any effective leader, as they are signs of high workplace and emotional intelligence.[*]

So, what's missing? Empathy is what's missing.

Without empathy, senior tech managers often don't know how to build trust and the cultures where people can thrive. In turn, teams don't believe management's agenda is in the team's best interests, and therefore don't trust *them.*

[**]See Hughes and Bradberry's book *The Emotionally Intelligent Team*

How can someone lead a successful team without understanding the viewpoints of the customer, the team members, or the competition?

When you don't know how to lead, when you can't build trust with lower hierarchy levels—and when you micromanage—people will distrust you. I was exactly that way as the leader on my first major project. I grew beyond that, but many don't.

Many senior managers are really only interested in the technology. What qualifies them to be in their roles? Why are they responsible for the lives and performance of hundreds of people? Good questions.

Also, they may not understand or acknowledge the role that other people play in *their* success. This is endemic, of course.

Here's a good example from outside the tech world. An esteemed surgeon I've known for years related to me how little he and his team felt trusted by their hospital management. This was true even though he and his team were in many ways the profit drivers for the hospital.

He also mentioned a "God complex" where some doctors assume they are the smartest people in every room and don't seem able to understand their patients or coworkers as people. No empathy. Some tech managers share this "God complex," and the inability to understand their employees as individuals.

To sum up our understanding of senior managers, they are smart and accomplished. They are in many ways special; the best of the best. They make a lot of money. Almost no one questions them, tells them they're wrong. They just haven't learned how to lead people. A shame.

They need to not distrust empathy and other "soft" skills. **Empathy is a tool by which you can achieve success through an understanding of your people**. Awareness and appreciation of that fact is a start. I understand this may be a bit like getting bulls to sit down for tea.

I believe empathy is what enables us to work successfully with each other. I simply cannot imagine functioning as a person in any effective way without empathy.

Senior managers should learn to talk with people from where the people themselves are coming from, then match their management style with what it takes to help those people succeed. Until they can learn to do so, these managers run the risk of being mistrusted and thus less effective.

Passionate is Just Another Word for Let Me Control You

Leaders with toxic behaviors thrive on controlling people instead of inspiring them.
—Simon Sinek, author, motivational speaker, and business consultant

Freedom's just another word for nothing left to lose.
—Kris Kristofferson, musician

The Issue:

I know you've heard the Kris Kristofferson song "Me and Bobbie McGee." The most famous version of the song might be Janis Joplin's, but Kris sounds good singing it too. My favorite line from that song is quoted above.

Often, management tries to control you by saying things like, *"We want people who are passionate about our mission around here."* Then they make you prove it without ever saying what they will do to help *you* succeed.

Often they ask you to:

- Work 100+ hours per week.
- Take any kind of verbal or mental abuse they want to lay on you.
- Find ways to get work done with broken or half-working tools.
- Deliver the product and then deal with finding a new job after they RIF you.

It's not about growing the skills of a team or individuals. They just want to use you and the minions to create *their* successful futures.

Dealing With the Issue:

You deal with this by not buying into their vision. Ask the right questions, such as "What's the culture like here?" and "What is your retention rate?" BEFORE you take the job.

Check Glassdoor or other apps to see what ex-employees say. Get on the right Reddit board to educate yourself.

Have the courage not to accept a position that may be in the wrong organization. There are some places that do it right. Find one!

You Can't Trust These People, You Know

The Issue:

In a previous book, I wrote about conversations with senior managers and their belief that development teams can't be trusted to tell the truth. Why they go to all the trouble to hire the best technical talent they can find and then immediately begin to doubt the talent's veracity probably says more about the senior manager than it does about the talent.

When they don't trust others and aren't trusted themselves, many senior managers will impose added control, such as more metrics, more reviews, planned tiger teams with team leaders, whatever they might come up with.

It's understandable to a point, especially if control is the only tool in your tool box. I did the same things in "Zealot Failure."

A story may best illustrate this. I once took a consulting gig with a small start-up. The CEO was the kind of person who heard only what he wanted to hear, and he promised investors and potential customers a worldwide streaming event for an upcoming product. The target date was less than two months away.

The team was stunned, they didn't know how they could possibly do what he'd promised in the short time remaining. I had a great ten-person interview with most of the team leadership, then a 1:1 with the CTO, who would be my manager. I really liked the team members and the challenge, and they liked me. I was neutral on the CTO, but liked the salary and the stock options that would vest in six months, so I took the position.

My manager, who worked at company headquarters three hours away, took me out to a nice street cart lunch and said, *"Get on top of this thing."* and he'd *"Be in touch."*

I started the day after Christmas, that's how little time we had. He called me that first night after work, and in a very friendly tone, asked, *"Have you figured out who is screwing things up down there? You can't trust them, you know."* He sounded serious, but I laughed it off as best I could, and said, *"Just getting to know them."*

When he called the second night with the same question, I began to be concerned. I said, *"They seem fine to me, Dan"* (not his real name).

The next night he called again and was borderline belligerent.

I repeated my previous statement. *"They all seem fine. Just a tough task."*

The fourth night he called yet again, the last call of that type. *"I want you to find out who is effing things up down there."* I said, concerned and a bit mystified, *"I can't see that anyone is blocking me down here. It's a good team. We are working well together. I think we have a really good chance of making it."*

Dealing With the Issue:

As the team leader, you own the culture on your team. No one else.

Given only six weeks, I focused the team with a brief daily stand-up meeting that drove a once weekly team leaders review where we looked at the current state of the streaming frame. It all came down to trust and matching my leadership approach to the situation and the team. It worked.

The day after the prototype software was successfully demonstrated on schedule to Dan, I was let go. No vested stock options and no long-term contract. I was paid well for what I did.

The worldwide streaming event was successful.

It would be easy for me to tell you just don't get into a situation like this, that I was a putz who probably let his guard down in the interview process. The mistakes I did make were to discount the CEO and the CTO (my boss). They seemed so goofy. I just hadn't believed the CTO thought the team was the problem. How ridiculous.

But life is to be lived and I'd rather do interesting work than stagnate. I was fascinated to have only six weeks to help the team get the streaming platform ready. The team had no idea how to pull it off. I had some ideas, and I really liked the team.

The only advice I can offer here is don't make these mistakes, but do seek and enjoy challenging work!

The next story deals with another reason why teams don't trust management.

Committing to Management

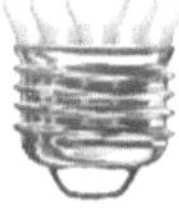

The best schedule is the one adapting to change.
—Tamerlan Kuzgov, author

The Issue:

In most organizations the schedule date is usually picked, i.e., committed to, by management. This means the development team is told the date to meet. The date chosen doesn't actually reflect whether the team can get that much work done by that date. In my view this is a major reason only 40% or so of projects in the tech world meet their schedules.

Here's how this type of "commitment" often goes:

- Senior manager(s) call the lead engineer(s)—no more than 2 people—into their offices.
- They effusively praise the lead engineer(s) to make them feel part of "the fraternity."
- With a wink and a nod, they say something like, "We need the Alpha Omega project to be done by X date. It'll look good to the customers and senior management if we can announce that now."
- The lead engineer(s) are not stupid. They know their next line in the script is something like "You bet!"
- But being honest engineers (virtually one-hundred percent of working level developers or engineers reflexively tell the truth) or maybe just to hedge their bets, they frown and say, *"That date's tough."*
- Management replies by saying, *"Oh, yeah, we know. But this date will keep the team focused and hungry."* Mostly it will just make the team cranky and stressed.

- The lead engineer(s) then say, *"We'll do our best."* You better believe they will bring this conversation up later when they start to slip schedule.

Everyone's fingers might as well be crossed behind their backs. None of them believe the date will be met, but the formalities have been followed. When the schedule is not met, house cleaning likely will occur, with the unpopular people or designated scapegoats being blamed and the golden-haired folks praised as "working really hard against tough odds."

Some other reasons why so many schedules committed to by management aren't met:

- The scope changes as the project progresses, generally increasing in complexity and cost. The scope changes aren't negotiated along the way as changes occur. Why? Generally from marketing pressures concerning a "market window." Sometimes this is valid; sometimes not so much.
- Management, not trusting the task leader's staffing plans, will generally under-staff the project in the beginning, thus making the situation worse later.

Creating new tech is hard enough without having one hand tied behind your back, so the team starts out demoralized and non-trusting.

Dealing with the Issue:

So, how to commit properly to management as a team? You start with the desired end date[*], working backwards from there in two-week milestones to eventually wind up at a more realistic end date to commit the team to.

You and the team thus have a reasonable schedule which is explainable to all. You and the team have told the truth. Stand up to any push-back. Perform. Works like a charm.

[**] See "Scheduling for Success" in Chapter 8 for more detail on the process.

Detecting BS Artists

The Situation:

It's the look in their eyes, as much as anything else. Most people are not good enough actors to be able to fool you if you look closely and know what to look for.

There will be a coldness in their eyes—the look one of envy, curiosity, or hostility—that a simple smile or slick kind-sounding words won't hide. This coldness reveals the calculation that is going on underneath. They never say anything truly positive and are often highly judgmental.

Authentic people have a light in their eyes—curiosity at times, but never envy or hostility, and they offer true support and helpful suggestions. Authentic people don't have to try to look powerful, they simply are powerful because of the approach they take.

The best leaders tell the truth. People can feel the truth in their words.

BS artists try to command the room and they work on people's fears. They are looking for ways to trip you up, control you, or find a way to control the situation to their advantage.

Dealing with the Situation:

I found many more authentic people in the world than I did BS artists, but there were a few everywhere I went. What to do when you run across a BS artist? Once you've confirmed a person is a BS artist, be careful, watch your flanks, and never take them into your confidence. Be confident in yourself, don't get caught up in their verbal traps. Be polite and businesslike. Ignore their jibes and build a network of trust with as many authentic people as you can.

"No one has the time, need, or interest in management practices or improvement processes."

Hundred-Person Wall Problem

When teams are quite small–say less than ten members–everyone gets to know everyone else well enough so that the culture, "a set of informal standard behaviors and actions to follow," develops quickly and organically. No one has the time, need, or interest in "management practices" or "improvement processes."

I worked with a few start-ups. Start-ups struggle repeatedly with the confusion and disarray that occurs as the company grows quickly. This is so frequent it has a name: "The Hundred-Person Wall."

Phil Wheat, a CTO told me: *"I've been involved in three start-ups and every one of them hit a wall right around one hundred employees. All of a sudden, what had been a fun place to work seemed much less fun, it was harder to get stuff done. Top people would leave to find that fun atmosphere again somewhere else."*

"Not just a hundred-person wall," said Jay Martin, CEO of an Internet of Things (IOT) start-up, *"It occurs at all growth spurts. There are walls that are hit at every growth spurt in start-ups, from 2 people to 5, from 5 to 20, 20 to 50, 50 to 100, 100 to 500. That's a real issue."*

Jeff Carter, an angel investor, in a blog titled: "Start-up Company Transition," wrote *"Once you get over 100 employees…you are no longer doing the fun product things…you are simply managing people."* An interesting way of showing how undervalued leading, as opposed to managing people, can be.

Why does this "Hundred-Person Wall" exist? Here is a nerdy scientific answer. Metcalfe's Law, which states that the number of unique connections in a network with number of nodes (n) (in this case n is the number of employees) can be expressed mathematically as proportional to n^2 asymptotically.

Huh? As you can see in the chart below, above 10 employees the rate of increase of interconnections increases dramatically, and beyond 50 employees the exponential effect really takes hold. We'll leave it at that.

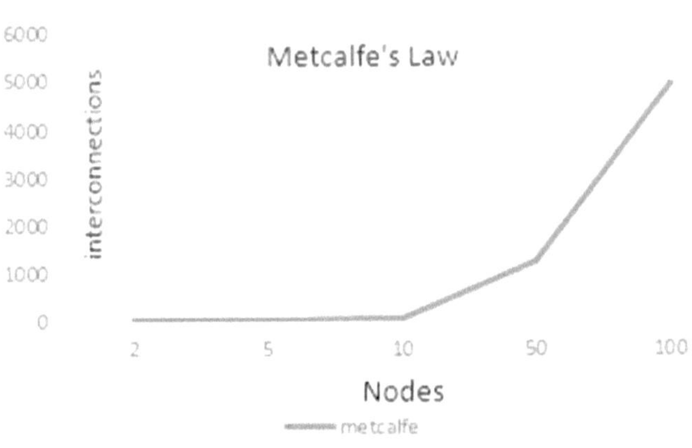

Figure created by author

Clearly, as the number of employees goes up, so does the need to communicate and the potential for confusion from so much data in the channel. New leadership skills are needed to deal with this. Simpler and more useful infrastructure and metrics are needed. Clever solutions, not bureaucracy.

Teams need to learn how to communicate without the direct and constant intervention of one brilliant creative genius acting as the center of the wheel. In start-ups, hundred-person wall confusion often results in a change-out in the entire management layer.

Seems awfully wasteful of human capital and destructive of relationships and embedded knowledge, but let's go with the assumption for the moment that in start-ups we've got to go *so* fast, be *so* nimble, and that our capital and time are *so* precious such that the hundred-person wall simply can't be dealt with any other way.

Nah. Just try the simple techniques in this book to increase the communication. Everyone tells the truth in this culture. In addition to communication and integrity, make sure your culture is based on accountability, trust, and transparency.

Teach your teams to use simple schedules, metrics, and risk logs (See Chapter 8) because, as Brian Joiner says in *Fourth Generation Management*, *"Teamwork is not something you command; it's something you foster by creating shared purpose and removing barriers."*

They Worry, You Know

The Issue:

In Chapter 6, I wrote about toxic managers who waste everyone's time and energy by calling tiger teams, by adding many new people at exactly the wrong time, or through any of the other games they play. These games destroy a team's cadence and rhythm. Why would people who've survived the gauntlet of tech, and who are smart and well educated, act this way?

Because they worry! They simply don't know what else to do. They use the tools they have, in this case, mostly just control.

And, similar to "Declaring Victory and Moving On," also from Chapter 6, there is a fair amount of cynicism present. They know their bosses are too busy to really figure out what they are doing well or poorly, so they try to do something that won't be easy to criticize, characterizing their actions as, "using my experience and wisdom to help the team where possible."

Many senior managers got to that level because they were able to get a flagship product out the door or an important process up and running in the fab—not because of their people skills—but because they could keep up with what everyone was doing better than the people actually doing the work could. The design manager in "No One Else in the Hospital" later in Chapter 7 was great at exactly that.

They were promoted for their technical skills, instead of the people leadership skills needed at those highly politicized senior levels. What these folks generally do is find someone they can trust and then support them through thick and thin, eventually getting a finished product. But it is often an ordeal.

In another example, from early in the manufacturing management phase of my career, I was assigned to a project that had spent a large amount (in the eight figures, I was told) of a military customer's money and had shipped very little to show for it.

There was a fair amount of urgency from division, engineering, and manufacturing management. I was told to go see the test technician *"down in the bone pile,"* in such and such area of the plant, and to get the product out.

"We'll want daily reports, probably up here face-to-face in the senior manager's office," they said. *"Sorta like a tiger team."* Ugh.

I found the tech and he showed me the bone pile. Sure enough, it was quite a pile of broken toys. Stuff was strewn everywhere. There were large sections of built-up printed-circuit-boards, some subsystems, and a few completed units, none of which had passed final test.

The tech and I talked, and came up with a plan. He would make a spreadsheet showing how many good boards we had of each type, the serial numbers of the boards that might make up complete units that we could send to final test along with the expected dates we could ship them, and the boards that failed repeatedly and seemingly couldn't be fixed. We would ask the customer for permission to use piece parts from those bad boards when troubleshooting failures. Pretty basic stuff, really. I told him I just wanted the facts. No BS.

Dealing with the Issue:

I knew senior management would want information by the end of that (and every subsequent) day, so I asked the tech to send me his spreadsheet by four PM. I gussied the spreadsheet up a bit, bolded a few items, wrote a one-paragraph summary, and emailed it to the key senior managers at roughly five o'clock, which was the time I thought they would come up for air from their afternoon meetings and therefore want status.

Any later would run the risk of them assuming the worst, and my being summoned to some sort of uncomfortable grilling. A few minutes later, I called the top guy and asked if he wanted me to come up to his office. *"Nope,"* he said. *"This looks good for now. We'll meet on Fridays every week."*

After that, every day at about five, I sent an updated spreadsheet in a format that showed that day's work, and cumulative work against the previous day's cumulative total. Steady progress was seen. We never had a face-to-face meeting. They had what they needed in order to quit worrying.

What can you do to minimize management's tendency to worry? Get them the right info; info they find trustworthy, that's what. We ultimately shipped enough units to satisfy the customer, that is, we gave them hardware they could show *their* management.

Just gather the facts. Part of doing so is evaluating your management's qualities and what will satisfy them.

Don't just ask them, they may not know and this might put them on the spot. Show them a format with the data they really need and they will go find other problems (they have several, always) to focus on.

It really is that simple.

"Sometimes improvement of one type or another is achieved, but it almost never lasts."

Eight Reasons Results Don't Sustain

Our tendency is to try things out capriciously. . .without an in-depth grasp of their underlying foundation, and without the commitment necessary to sustain them. When a new idea fails, we give up instead of investigating the causes of failure and addressing them systematically.
—Richard Tanner Pascale, author Managing on the Edge

The Issue:

Ineffective senior managers frequently push new initiatives onto their organizations exactly as Richard Pascale writes above. Sometimes improvement of one type or another is achieved, but it almost never lasts.

The manner in which these new initiatives are introduced often looks like this:

- The Senior Management Team discusses the need for change/improvement at a staff meeting (or, more likely, several), **then**
- Appoints a special committee to investigate potential programs and costs, **which then**
- Comes back with proposals for any one of a number of continuous improvement or Agile methodologies.

After this:

- One proposed process or another is chosen, **and**
- Extremely articulate trainer(s) are hired to come in generally for 3 to 5 days to teach the chosen process to a team or teams, **then**
- The trainers, paid nicely, leave and go on to their next assignment.
- Pilot project(s) are picked (often a showcase loaded with a team of the best employees), and the chosen process is implemented.

- Initial enthusiasm is sustained by early adopters, or process introduction coaches (sometimes called Black Belts or Scrum Masters) christened from within or hired into the organization.

Some change for the better may - probably does - occur. Someone may even get promoted (see "Declaring Victory and Moving On" in Chapter 6). Any of these processes/approaches can be instrumental in changing the culture and helping the organization become more effective at meeting its mission and satisfying its customers.

But, but, but...Wait. Fast forward six months to a year.

It is all too likely that management may now be reviewing metrics that show the organization has stopped improving or maybe even slipped back to the sorry state when the initial change was made.

Everyone involved sincerely wanted change to occur. How can this be? Why aren't the improvements sustainable?

The eight reasons results don't sustain:

1. The introduced process was chosen by a collection of senior people at too high a level in the organization to match the process with the working level details.
2. The internal coaches also didn't know these details.
3. The working level *did* know the details, but they were busy getting the job done, or had been working on management's "process of the month." In their minds the new process was nice, but it wasn't going to fix *their* problems. But no one asked them.
4. The trainers were now training others elsewhere.
5. Management's attention was now focused on a hundred other things.
6. Internal coaches and team leaders don't fully understand/appreciate the politics and the short attention span of the upper levels. Thus, they aren't able to effectively drive the needed actions.
7. Basic gaps in understanding/expectations around deeply rooted cultural issues that must be addressed before real change can "stick" have not been understood, and therefore sustainable change doesn't occur.

8. Management, coaches, team leaders, and working level team members don't know how to bridge these gaps. They may not even be consciously aware the gaps exist. After all, you can't fix what you're not aware of.

Dealing with the Issue:

Find what works for you. For example, 5S works great in a manufacturing environment, but not so well in engineering or design. Imagine telling technical people to clean up their work space.

Personally, I generally suggest pieces of several processes tailored to the team. Do not be driven by shifting corporate winds.

"There are few things worse than not being allowed to do a project your way and then being held accountable for the results."

Kill Me Now

[Sometimes]... the strong give up and move on, while the weak give up and stay
—Hall and Oates in song "Do What You Want, Be What You Are"

The Issue:

There are few things worse than not being allowed to do a project your way and then being held accountable for the results. Senior managers believe they are the smartest people in the room on most topics, and think they know best how to lead your teams successfully.

In that they are often wrong. Most senior managers do not understand how to schedule, to use metrics effectively, or to motivate a team-in other words how to lead. They love and understand their technical specialty, but to them the management stuff is a drag. Several have told me exactly so in a moment of candor.

Dealing with the Issue:

A variation on the following conversation occurred more times than I can remember.

Them: *"I don't understand why you want to do that."*

Me: *"Because it's what needs to happen."*

Them: *"I don't like it. Doesn't seem right to me."*

Me: Long pause. It's time to say the words. *"Kill me now, then."*
Them: Incredulous. *"What?"* Remember they are smarter than me, at least in their minds.

Me: *"Kill me now. Don't make me live through it and then kill me. Doing it your way will not work. Either I have the leeway to do things my way or I don't. If you can do my job, do it."*

Sometimes I would offer to hand them my badge. I admit that was overly dramatic.

Them: Hard glance at me. *"You're serious?"*

Me: *"Yep. Very."*

Them: Pause. Another hard glance. *"Go ahead, then. Do it."*

Me: Nod. *"Thanks."* And I would.

A caveat. Only do the above if:

- You can look absolutely serious and quite stern.
- You have a reputation for being successful with teams.
- You have an understanding partner at home.

I believe the risk of getting fired or reassigned is worth it for, lack of a better word, your soul. After all, why live through your project being done the wrong way, and then get yourself killed for the inevitable failure? Better to make a change and move on to something that has a chance to succeed. By the way, no one ever let me give them my badge.

No One Else in the Hospital

The Issue:

For starters, the most senior of my new employees said, *"It would be great if no one else had to go to the hospital."*

She was replying to my question, *"What would you like to see change around here?"* Turns out one of the team members had been to the hospital and a second member was having stress related stomach aches and was well on her way there.

I had just been hired to head the project management section for a very large design team at a major semiconductor company. I was meeting with each of my new employees to get the lay of the land.

I next had several one-on-one meetings with the head of the project. There I found the source of most of the stress mentioned by my employee. Turns out senior managers *can* create such toxic cultures that the employee's health *is* affected. I was told by the head of the project several times that I needed to *"Do what I was told."* I realized my work was cut out for me.

I listened without much response but eventually I tried to explain my approach. She didn't respond. She reminded me that my several previous predecessors had only been retained for something like a year each.

To be fair, this individual was under enormous stress to get a microprocessor design out on time. In addition, who knows what horrors she encountered as a woman in a male-dominated field.

The project management team was composed of excellent analysts being made sick (literally) by this well-meaning, but overly demanding senior manager. The information our project management team gathered was excellent. They were viewed as the honest brokers on the project by the project head, who was extremely distrustful of almost everyone. She didn't trust us much either, just more so than the others.

My team had been over-driven by her. Their scope of work (her expectations) changed daily, sometimes several times a day. Combine the overbearing and punishing personality of the project head with the people-pleasing perfectionism of my team, in an environment of high stress, and you have a recipe for disaster.

Dealing with the Issue:

I made it my job to become the buffer between my team and the rest of the project. I set boundaries for engagement and interaction. I told the project head that I couldn't do my job if she tasked my team whenever and for whatever she felt like. I reiterated our team's desire to give her and the project what they needed.

I asked for a list of weekly deliverables. As always, my team would continue to answer any questions or investigate extra work, as long as there was available time for the standard weekly deliverables.

My direct line manager supported me. But, of course, if my release had been demanded, my manager would have had no choice but to do so.

Once a quarter my manager's boss would fly in from western vistas for a couple of days to see how we were doing. He would meet 1:1 with me, my boss, the design manager, and my team. The first evening he would take those of us in his organization out to eat sushi. Always had to be sushi.

After eighteen months or so, he said to me, *"Doug, I don't know exactly what you've done here, but it is now a pleasure to visit the site. Your team is so much happier; no gloom and doom!"* Along the way I had been offered a promotion to a position in California, but since our kids were in their critical middle school years, soon to enter high school, I reluctantly declined.

Oh, yes. He never mentioned any complaints from engineering. That is a key reason I felt she was only trying to control me, and wasn't serious about offing me. After several months of weekly one-on-one meetings with me, she said, *"Doug, you don't need to meet with me anymore. You don't listen to me."* I did listen, just didn't obey too well. I was relieved.

I didn't argue. I smiled briefly and said, *"OK, if, you're sure."*

"I am sure," she said.

How did things turn out? The project finished successfully. The Project Head was promoted to VP. And no one else went to the hospital!

"In the defense industry—unlike the semiconductor industry—a program manager (as opposed to a design manager) is actually an important job."

Snake Pits

The Issue:

In the defense industry—unlike the semiconductor industry—a program manager (as opposed to a design manager) is actually an important job. The job is viewed as a stepping stone to section or division management. Virtually every senior manager in our government/defense sector started as a PM.

The PM is responsible for winning the contract, executing it successfully with the team while also maintaining good government and corporate customer relations, and reporting up through a complicated senior management hierarchy.

As I said, project management is viewed very differently in the commercial tech world (perhaps that is why PM is generally done so poorly there), almost as glorified schedulers or as people "not technical enough" for real engineering work. Not the point at all.

When I first became a project manager in the defense sector an old head, let's call him Fred, stopped me in the hall. Poor Fred was shrunken with testicular cancer and very ill. He was a ghost of a man. After congratulating me on getting the job, Fred asked me how old I was.

"Thirty-five," I said.

"Young for the job," he said. *"It's a snake pit, you know. We'll see how long you last. I lasted six years."*

I just looked at Fred and smiled. I knew better! I was going places, by gosh!

I lasted six years in the job, just like Fred.

Dealing with the Issue:

But I didn't sit by, fat, dumb and happy, waiting for a political sword to fall. Instead, I moved on to the commercial part of our corporation, where my experience in team leadership proved very beneficial.

There I was the adult in the room. I was able to notice issues endemic to leading project teams, whether in defense or commercial semiconductor design. Several issues seem to pop up over and over again no matter where you are. I've captured many of those issues in this book.

All jobs can be *"snake pits."* They are what you make them.

Pain Avoiding Animals

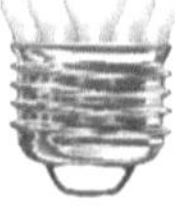

The Issue:

This story covers more than just the behavior of ineffective managers. All levels of people can do really dumb things in respect to raising problems or issues; behavior that often goes against their own best interests. We've all seen it. But why?

Simple: people are pain avoiding animals.

We ask our spouses, our friends, our kids: "What issues need fixing?" Their response to that question is often innocuous and unhelpful. For example, your spouse may not want to potentially start an argument or hurt your feelings, so they soft soap the answer. Result: You learn nothing substantive. They avoid potential pain this way. Thus, pain avoiding animals.

In a tech team setting, this behavior is wide spread. First of all, developers and engineers tend to be introverts and perfectionists. As an introvert myself, I can tell you nothing wears me out more than having a discussion that I strongly suspect will be useless in generating substantive action. Rope-A-Dope specialists, as mentioned in "Dougisms" in Appendix D, rely on this.

Perfectionism can lead to shame when problems occur. Rather than raising the issue for solution, team members may just keep it hidden. Especially in the shame-based cultures that are so present these days.

Maybe they think they or their sub-team can fix the problem before anyone finds out. Just easier to BS through it, as they see it. After all, they see their management do that on a frequent basis. Again, pain avoiding animals.

Dealing with the Issue:

Being aware of this tendency in people has saved me a lot of trouble over the years. Technical people have few communication issues among people they trust. For example, teams of testers or developers, working in small specialty teams, communicate just fine. Yes, they argue and release emotion. That is a good thing. Bottling up important feelings and thoughts is what shame-based culture is all about. They get along just fine and talk in detail with those they trust. And best yet, they make decisions.

In the proper context, and with reasonable guidelines and guardrails, I never had a problem getting my teams to open up about what was wrong. Quite the contrary. Once they realized I was actually there to help, some of them actually *over* communicated. See the story in Chapter 5 "In a Sentence, Please."

Don't play games. Just tell the truth. If you make a mistake, fess up. You may have to take a beating on occasion. None of us are perfect, and we all mess up once in a while, and probably deserve to hear about it.

Just don't become so averse to personal pain that you become less adventurous and eventually stale. As Israeli Prime Minister Golda Mier said, *"Trust yourself. Create the kind of self that you will be happy to live with all your life. Make the most of yourself by fanning the tiny, inner sparks of possibility into flames of achievement."*

CHAPTER EIGHT

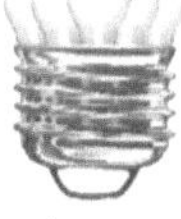

Schedules and Other Required Stuff

When you get right down to it, one of the most important tasks of a leader is to eliminate his people's excuse for failure.
— Robert Townsend, best-selling author and executive

Failure is central to engineering. Successful engineering is all about understanding how things break or fail.
—Henry Petroski, author of many books on engineering as a discipline

Schedules, risk logs, metrics, and periodic reviews are necessary evils. The use of these tools can provide the information you need to be successful. This chapter is meant to show you how to use them better.

"I was hired into an organization that was in a bind. Actually, this sentence could start several of these stories."

Scheduling for Success

The key is not to prioritize what's on your schedule, but to schedule your priorities.
—Stephen Covey, author of The Seven Habits of Highly Effective People

I was hired into an organization that was in a bind* They were under incredible pressure to deliver a micro-processor core for a chip going to our corporation's 800-pound cellular phone gorilla.

I was fortunate to work with some great people on the team, starting with the engineering project manager, Brian. After listening to my approach, he and his senior leadership team agreed to try it.

I suggested that eight to ten people (him, me, and his key staff) take a couple of hours a day for a week or so—away from all the distractions—to milestone plan the schedule. The deliverable was due roughly nine months in the future. I told them to forget about that for the moment.

I said we were going to plan from the end. Why do that? Because the content of the work was fairly well understood by the team, and planning backwards took away the perfectionist tendency that drives developers and engineers to freeze—to lock up—when creating a schedule.

We would call the delivery date Day zero. I asked the group: *"What's the thing that has to happen about two weeks before the delivery date?"* Their response: *"Tasks to prepare the code for shipment."*

"OK," I said, writing down what they had said, *"what about two weeks before that, what has to happen?"* And on we went, backwards from there, all the way to "Now." Only then did we look at how long it actually took.

This approach took a lot of stress out of the perfectionist technical people, including the developers, design engineers, architects, and me.

**Actually, this sentence could start several of these stories.

We really want to do things right, really want to be successful, so if we try to schedule from the beginning, we often have difficulty covering *everything* and lock up.

The schedule duration for the microprocessor core we came up with was six or so weeks later than the nine months demanded. There was some consternation about the date not being what management and the internal customer had demanded. This is when—and only when—I said, *"We don't necessarily accept the date that comes down from management. Those are political dates. They aren't real performance dates. There are all sorts of agendas embedded in those scheduling dates."* Some bright and intrigued eyes were watching me. The meeting adjourned.

Brian waited until everyone else had left and said, *"We gotta' talk."* And talk we did, in my office (so no one could find him in his office). Brian said, *"We're pushing the limits of what management will tolerate, maybe beyond."*

Here's where some calculation (emotional intelligence sounds less Machiavellian) was needed. I said, *"here's the calculation. They won't fire you for this. You are a golden-haired boy."* He nodded. Indeed true.

I continued. *"And they won't fire me, a so-called expert on doing this sort of thing, because they just spent a small fortune moving me, my family, and all our junk across the country. Firing me now would look weak. You and me will never be stronger. If you accept their mandated date, we will never have the chance to do this again."* (see "Kill Me Now.")

He agreed. We took the two-week milestone schedule to management. All hell broke loose when we told them the date we would commit to. Two months late, (six weeks actually) they said. An outrage! One local customer demanded our heads.

We were quickly called into the office of the two Senior VPs who ran the entire design organization, not just our little piece. The most senior of them was Tom Gunter, who, according to Bradford Morgan White in *Abort Retry Fail,* his ambitious Substack post, *"[was] the father of the Motorola 68000, which along with its descendants would be used in essentially everything that wasn't an IBM compatible for a long time."*

According to Gunter's 2024 obituary, *"The microprocessor became one of the most instrumental processors developed during the dawn of the personal computing age, and was featured on the cover of National Geographic for its significance to the industry and to the launch of the Apple Macintosh in 1984."*

We showed them our work and our backup data, then we explained how we derived our schedule. They asked some reasonable questions, probing our logic and understanding. When they were through, they said, *"We'll support you."* Just like that.

Credit to them. If they hadn't, we would have been in a real pickle. I think they reacted so reasonably because they could tell that we knew what we were doing, and trusted us. I think they were in charge for a good reason.

Ultimately, **we shipped on the date we had committed to**. Our core then **sat on the shelf for almost a year** at the local customer's site before the rest of the chip was ready. Needless to say, our local customer didn't complain anymore about us.

Promotions and raises occurred. Brian moved higher elsewhere in the org. Tom Gunter left and the other SVP, Dave Mothersole, was given seven design groups to integrate into one huge organization. In his words, *"I was hired to be the adult in the room"* to do what I had done in the one design team for all seven organizations.

Managing the schedule afterwards...

I told the sub-teams they could build whatever schedule they wanted to underneath the initial milestones, as long as overall we managed to the milestones list. The milestone list status is what I reported to management.

I tried hard to prevent the sub-team schedules from coming up for detailed discussion in management reviews. Too detailed and way too many opportunities for micro-management, chest-pounding contests, and other non-value-added time wasters.

How much time did I spent on the schedule in an average week?

- Part of an hour in each team meeting.
- I'd update the detailed schedule by talking to people, and that, along with calculating the Earned Value (see story in this chapter) once per week, would take a couple of hours.
- I would spend a mostly pleasant hour per month at project reviews. We never reported schedule variance (nerd speak for being late).

That's it. Maybe four hours a week, on average.

Team's response to schedule approach...

I think most everyone enjoyed the milestone schedule's creation. They didn't sandbag; they got to discuss issues and then decide what the milestones were. It worked for them.

Unmangling the Metrics

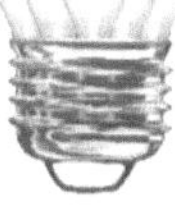

What gets measured gets done, what gets measured and fed back gets done well, what gets rewarded gets repeated.
—Lawyer, John E. Jones III

Metrics measure project performance from various aspects, and have been required on every project I've ever been involved with. Most organizations have a standard list of metrics, often influenced or even created by the latest improvement "program of the month." These lists can be capricious and the choices for what's included can lack common sense.

Metrics can be quite dangerous in tech projects, as trends in the metrics can be used to support arguments, from whichever agenda one holds, concerning how the project is going. There were so many metrics being discussed in most organizations that a case could be made for anything. Maybe *that* was the real agenda.

A case could be made for:

- We're on an uptrend; therefore, we're doing fine.
- Yes, we're on a downtrend, but here's why we're really doing fine.
- Yes, the project is on a downtrend and things look bad, but it is not my department's fault.

Get the picture?

And I would sit there and wonder, is this confusion what management actually wants? There *are* a lot of different agendas in those rooms.

Some potential agendas around the table:

- I want things to get worse so I can get more resources for my team.
- Maybe I can get rid of a certain person in a certain position.
- I want to show things are getting better because it's my group.

- I want to show it's getting better because we made an investment last year in my group, and I want to show that it got a return so that I get credit.

Everyone wants the business to be successful, but those are real human agendas from ambitious human beings.

Everybody wants to win the basketball championship every year, too, but don't get to because their team doesn't play well, or doesn't have the right people. I wanted every project to win its particular championship, so I had to learn how to handle the metrics craziness. An edited example from an old real unnamed project will illustrate. See Figure 8-1 below.

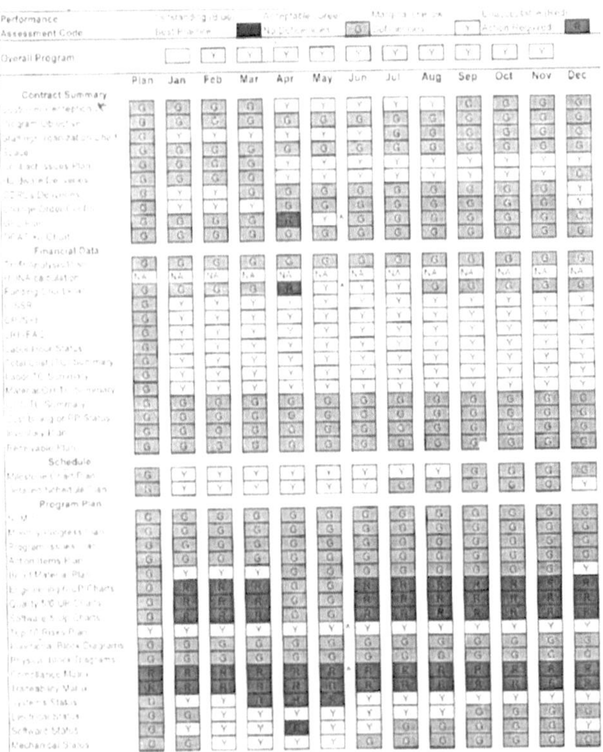

Figure 8-1: Generic Motorola Project Status Chart
(Author's Depiction)

Nightmare of confusion. So much data, what is one to make of this? Are things going well or poorly? Well, there's a lot of red and yellow, so things must be bad, eh? But there's also a lot of green. The first line shows the customer is happy, but then down the page it looks like costs are a bit out of control (C/SSR, et al), and further down, it shows the engineering 6-Up Charts are red! Different organizations graded different metrics, with each organization clearly mired in their own agendas.

If you are the person ostensibly in charge of the overall project, what should you do?

I would briefly present the list and status of the required metrics. I would then show a second slide with the five or so metrics the engineering team and I thought were the most important. During the briefing I'd look over at the senior engineer team members and get nods, *"Yep, those are the important ones."*

Which metrics from the list are the most important? Depends on the project, and that can vary month to month. Your only agenda as the leader is to report the true status from the perspective of meeting the organization's goals.

A couple of points. I would almost always include the Top Risks, Customer Perception, Profit and Schedule, plus any from the list that had been red status for a long time if they really mattered.

Generally, management's attention span won't be long while you're talking, and they will focus on whatever hot buttons they have at that moment. Of course, they'll interrupt and you'll have to let them talk until they are done. Just be ready with your key two or three sentence talking points to sum up.

Another thing about metrics. People will find out what is being watched closest, and they will perform to those metrics. So, to make everyone's life easier, you should push (sell) the importance of the metrics the team cares about and would manage to if left to their own devices.

"EVM is an objective way of measuring the progress of a project against its plan.."

Earned Value Management

EVM is an objective way of measuring the progress of a project against its plan. All defense development contracts of sufficient complexity require Earned Value Management (EVM).

I was therefore considered an expert on EVM when I came to the semiconductor side with seventeen years of experience in defense projects. Almost no one in semiconductor had ever heard the term.

Thus, one of the first tasks I undertook in the semiconductor world was explaining and implementing earned value on the microprocessor development project I was hired to lead.

You can find an almost endless supply of books, articles, and consulting companies on EVM. It is very easy to get wrapped around the earned value axle in the defense world, but I knew it would have to be simple and straightforward if the semiconductor development team was going to accept it. Also, many games are played in defense with EVM, and I wanted to avoid those.

Three components, which must be calculated and compared against each other are shown in Figure 8-2.

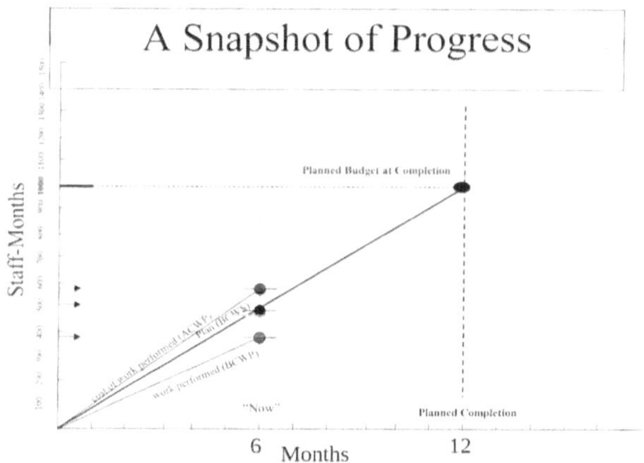

Figure 8-2
(author's work)

The plan, the Budgeted Cost of Work Scheduled (BCWS);

The earned value, which measures how much work has been done. This is the Budgeted Cost of Work Performed (BCWP);

The cost of **the work accomplished**, called Actual Cost of Work Performed (ACWP)

The figure shows a hypothetical project at Month 6 of a planned twelve-month duration. To make sense of how we are doing on this project, two more odd sounding terms must be introduced.

- Cost Variance (CV), the difference between the work performed (BCWP) and the actual cost (ACWP), CV= BCWP – ACWP. A positive CV means the project's work performed is more than the cost planned for that work. This is good.
- Schedule Variance (SV), the difference between the work performed (BCWP) and the work planned (BCWS), or SV = BCWP – BCWS. A positive SV means the project's work performed is more than the amount of work scheduled. This also is good.

We can now estimate the current schedule slippage, the planned budget at completion, the projected completion date, and the projected overall project schedule slippage and any cost overrun, as shown on the following chart.

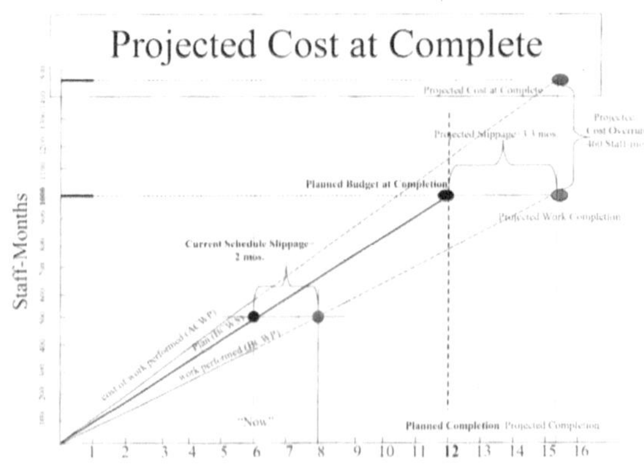

Figure 8-3
(author's work)

Of course, this is a simplified example, as the planned work, cost of work, and work performed are all linear from project start to finish. But the technique used to project final performance from the month 6 actuals is accurate. The projected variances shown (schedule slippage of 3.3 months and cost overrun of 460 man-hours) should drive common-sense mitigation plans and work-arounds in month 6 intended to shrink these variances before completion.

To do EVM in semiconductor:

- The 0/100 rule was instituted, where tasks got 0% credit when started, and 100% task credit only at task completion.
- No task would be longer than two weeks. Tasks longer than that had to be split up into two-week chunks.
- A realistic schedule was the goal. This meant a schedule the team built, believed in, and would support. And could reasonably meet.
- Conservative resource (people) loading. No one had tasks totaling more than 100% of a work week. No babies, as it were, in one month.
- The project would be run the way it had been planned.

It worked great and we used it successfully seven times over the three years it was used.

"Getting along with people is key to all of this. The goal is to not get yourself into a lose-lose position or become the designated scapegoat."

Creepy Scope

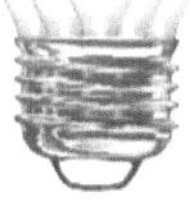

Expect the best, plan for the worst, and prepare to be surprised.
–Denis Waitley, motivational speaker, writer and consultant

In "Committing to Management" in Chapter 7, I wrote how project scope always seems to increase over time. Poor managers will insist that you absorb the extra scope in your schedule without shifting the commitment date. Not fair.

I've heard many variations of the following statements, along with angry glares directed at me from senior manager. *"You're just playing games!* This is tech. Everyone knows the definition of the tasks is going to change over time." True, I am sure.

That statement is why managing scope, frankly, is creepy. Creepy as in creeping, and creepy as in downright strange. Keeping track of the scope agreed to is critical to you and the team's success. For example, I twice managed contracts in the defense sector where the requirements changed so much that the contract values grew by over 100%. Not bloat from our team, just a customer who kept changing the specifics of what they wanted. We wouldn't have gotten paid the full amount if we hadn't documented the scope changes adequately.

No one in commercial tech likes to talk scope. *"Too anal,"* they'll say, *"This is BS. Just suck it up and get it done."* **Part of your job is to be the team's advocate and refuse to take on additional scope without schedule relief or additional resources, be they the right people or tools.**

This can be a real battle. The statements from senior managers above, as far as they go, are correct in a certain way. But where do you draw the line? When do you say no, and when do you wiggle, or compromise, or nod your head and agree? A CEO and multi-book author once called me the toughest negotiator he had ever worked with so I offer the following.

Scope negotiating tactics:

- **Nodding your head and agreeing**. Management and everyone else need to know you aren't playing games. You shouldn't have brought the issue up if you weren't on firm ground. But sometimes you'll bring up an issue and after hearing the push back your certainty may soften. In this case maybe you nod your agreement. You might even say something like, *"I'll go with you on this one, but let's both remember this. Maybe it will be my turn next time."*
- **Wiggle.** In this context wiggle means to engage in conversation until you determine how serious the other side is about the issue under discussion. Management will use the standard statements mentioned above anytime you bring up scope creep. Push back and talk it over with them a bit until you determine how important the issue is to them. This is not Rope-a-Dope because you are not trying to avoid the discussion/extra work. You are seeking to understand.
- **Compromise**. Sometimes you've got to give a little to get a little. Maybe both sides are making good points. Knowing when to do so and how to do so are what experience (and this book) can do for you. You need to realize that while you want the org to win—no matter what senior management may think your motivations are—you also want to protect the team and give them the chance for their hard work to succeed. Balancing those two facets are the most important parts of your job.
- **Saying NO Diplomatically**. Best not to just say, *"No way."* That would make you quite unpopular and possibly weaken your position. Do so only when agreeing is an existential impact to the team's chance for success.

The best position to be in will come from saying something like, *"The team and you guys in senior management approved the schedule." All the major tasks were estimated by people who know the work. We can look at what can be dropped or minimized, if you like. But also, the org and all of us will look bad if we miss the schedule because of extra work. If a schedule slip works for you then sure, I guess that's the way to go."*

Saying no in this way can actually give senior management a way to get to a type of yes, to save face if you will. Much better politically for you.

Getting along with people is key to all of this. The goal is to not get yourself into a lose-lose position or become the designated scapegoat.

*"Work can be over planned and
it can be under planned.."*

Wrong Headed Planning

Work can be over planned and it can be under planned. Over planning in the tech world occurs when there are too many cooks in the kitchen. I worked[*] on a big satellite system for a commercial company that started out with the mindset "we need the minimum viable satellite that meets the mission requirements so we can keep weight and costs down."

But during the design phase they increasingly began to say things at the Change Control Board (I was there) like, *"We need that feature too, and that one, and that one."* Net result was they had to change the launch vehicle due to the extra weight of the satellite. Huge extra cost, and a schedule delay out the wazoo. An example of how a poor planning process impacted the implementation of a great idea.

Changing focus now, I suggest General George B McClellan *("I shall not move my Army until absolutely ready")* as an *over* planner par excellence. He was an acknowledged genius who seemingly excelled at everything he did. Entered West Point at fifteen, finished second in his class. Served with distinction in the Mexican-American War. Democratic presidential candidate in 1864. Governor of New Jersey. A very accomplished man. And the commanding general of the US Army from 1861-1862, when Lincoln finally removed him.

Why? Because he wouldn't engage the enemy, taking little action *except* planning. On and on, looking for the perfect plan.

On the under-planning side, General Ulysses S Grant *("If you see the President, tell him from me that whatever happens there will be no turning back")* was another matter entirely. He did very little planning. Instead, he analyzed the situation on the battlefield and adjusted his approach based on what he saw. As Grant said, *"In every battle there comes a time when both sides consider themselves beaten. Then he who continues the attack wins."* Like Patton in World War II, Grant's modus operandi was to push on.

[**]only as a cost analyst, no leadership role.

He *"hit 'em the "hardest with the most-est,"* a quote generally attributed to Confederate General Nathan Bedford Forrest. But *"Unconditional Surrender"* Grant, as he was nicknamed after victory at Fort Donelson, made it an art form. I do not believe he was a butcher. If you doubt me, go read some biographies on him. He did, however, put the metal down and GO!

Many senior managers want to do the exact same thing. Saves time, you see, on thinking and planning. But you wouldn't head off in a generally northeast direction without a map or GPS, would you, from Atlanta to New York City? Oh, you would? Better get going then. Good luck and go fast!

Hitting the enemy hard is done all the time, but is not so likely to work as well in tech. It worked for Grant because he had more men and resources at his disposal than did the South, and he was frankly smarter than the generals he faced, at least until Lee. Not so easy in tech, where there are lots of resources and many other companies, and many technically smart people.

Don't get me wrong: good planning is done by the Army[*], as well in Special Forces units, where management sets the objective, but not the tactics for a mission. This gives flexibility on the ground. Matching the approach to the situation is what this book is all about.

[**]I'm not familiar with US Navy and Air Force planning. That is why I use the US Army in the example.

Risk Management

Risk comes from not knowing what you're doing.
–Warren Buffet, Investor

Needless to say, Risk Management is a complicated subject. It is beyond the scope of this book to cover the subject from zero to full speed. However, I will give my viewpoint and try to give you enough resources to make the right decisions for your projects.

When you start the planning process for a project, one of the first things you need to think about is: what can go wrong? Issues will inevitably come up, and you need a mitigation strategy in place to know how to manage the risks when project planning.

But how do you work towards resolving the unknown? PMI and IEEE are great resources, and there is almost an endless supply of books on the subject. From the website of private company "PM Project Management's" website this quote is a great starting point: *"Project risk management is the process of* ***identifying, analyzing and responding*** *to any risk that arises over the life cycle of a project to help the project remain on track and meet its goal."* I have no business relationship, past or present, with the company.

Identifying, analyzing, and responding to risks is the effort I led in "No One Ever Asked Us Before" from Chapter 3. A more formalized approach to the same process was used to achieve a 6-sigma quality level on another manufacturing project I led in the same building, one of the few in the corporation.

I was also part of a team that published an article in an edition of the Intel Technology Journal entitled "Managing Product Development Risk."

Improvements will happen if important risks can be identified and mitigated before extra work, cost, and schedule delays occur.

Here are some benefits to actively managing risks that will help sell the process:

- **Customer Satisfaction.** Finding and fixing risks helps get new contracts or product sales.
- **Cost Avoidance.** Can be estimated by multiplying problems that have actually occurred within a 10- year period by the estimated cost of those repairs. You could then say with some believability that if X risks were mitigated, then Y cost of future repairs would be avoided.
- **Cost Reduction.** If the project is finished early, the organization will save a lot of money. This is especially true considering how many projects are actually late, with their *unplanned costs*, when compared against *savings* from being early. Active risk identification and mitigation could reasonably be credited with some of those savings.

De-activated Risk

This story is a successful example of active risk management, where looking ahead for potential risks saved us big bucks. Our engineering design manager had been closely monitoring the top ten risk list and this was instrumental in getting quick upper management approval for a large capital investment needed for additional server computing resources. These resources prevented a *coming* bottleneck in verification testing, which would have delayed the project.

This is a solid example of active risk management because several individuals and layers of team and senior management worked together (imagine that!), and did so because the risk was raised and then mitigated until removal, several months before the risk turned into reality.

"Whatever your organization requires create risk logs and stop-light charts and top five risk lists."

Un-agile AGILE

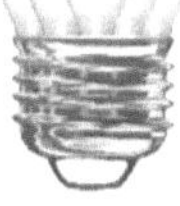

Agile is an attitude, not a technique with boundaries.
–Alistair Cockburn, author, *Manifesto for Agile Software Development*

Risk management seems pretty straightforward in manufacturing, as faults in soldering or part placement are just easier to find and fix than the amorphous bugs found in software.

One reason, certainly not the only one, is because Agile, which was meant to be an improvement process that was an "euonym" (a name well suited to the person, place, or thing), has become almost a religion unto itself, with rules that must be precisely followed or someone will protest it is not being done properly.

I am a certified scrum master, and that is not Agile in my mind, nor, it seems, in the mind of Alistair Cockburn, as quoted above. I have used the process several times. The following example from a small start-up shows why flexibility is required (even on Agile!).

As I always do, I matched the process used (a light process) to the team and the situation (a six-week delivery time with a spaghetti code baseline for a worldwide streaming event).

I instituted daily, 15-minute stand-up meetings where immediate problems that impeded progress were raised and actions assigned. Also, many 1:1s were held to remove roadblocks and to gain consensus. We did not vote 1, 3, 10 points on different stories (pieces of code or features). Bugs were tracked but this had no true value to me. There simply wasn't enough time. I would do more of that on a larger project, with a modified approach.

If you try to add too much process the team will rebel or under commit to the process. This is a **key tenet** to why I never had had a project that failed to meet its goals.

Whatever your organization requires, create risk logs and stop-light charts and top five risk lists. But always remember to evaluate the situation you and the team are in against which and how much process you use.

Meetings, Meetings, and More @#!$% Meetings

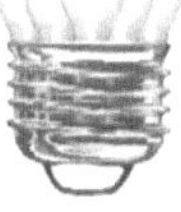

People who enjoy meetings should not be in charge of anything.
—Thomas Sowell, economist

Poor leadership has conditioned design teams, and others teams for that matter, to think all meetings are basically a waste of time. Therefore, these team members, being clever, resist *new* meetings.

To combat this, you should plan team meetings (or any other meeting) to go as quickly and get as much done as possible, and should do the following:

- Send out the agenda two or three days before the meeting. Having an agenda allows you to keep the meeting focused. Have an entry for "additional issues to discuss" on the agenda. Bullpen items and any new key issues raised in the meeting can go here.
- Always start and end on time. Strive to be five minutes early, and to be the first person present. Be the last person to leave by appearing to be making notes. Often, if people see you staying late, they will also stay behind to bring up something and you can learn important information.
- Don't waste the team's time on unnecessary personal rants. If you must rant, call a separate "Come to Jesus" meeting with the specific offending parties. This is showing consideration for non-involved people's time.
- One of the agenda items should be a review of the bullpen or bin list of deferred items from other meetings you've led.

At first, I got the same negative reactions mentioned earlier in this story. Over time, I developed an approach where I would talk to as many people on the team as possible, and then modify the organization's approach, be it AGILE or whatever, to the team and situation.

My suggestions would be based on what I thought was needed and what the team could endure, considering its past experience and maturity around things like schedule, risks, metrics, and meetings.

If team members gripe about attending *yet* another meeting, I say *"Fine. If you think it is a waste of time, don't come."* That makes them draw back in wonder, let me tell you.

Fortunately, there was always a quorum of problem-solvers attending, and attendance would improve as the team realized that problems were actually solved in those meetings. Eventually even the hardest hard heads didn't want to be left out.

We engineers are problem-solvers who think deeply about problems. Engineers and developers are smart, and are dedicated to doing a good job. However, engineers and developers also fiercely want their own work to be useful and used. They want their technology to take over the world. We come up with answers, and defend those answers passionately.

They are straight shooters on technical matters if they aren't concerned about the speaker being a politician or a management shill. In fact, basically only engineers with management potential are invited to meetings with customers, because your normal engineer is too honest, and will sometimes answer questions too clearly or with way too much detail, as opposed to saying a whole lot of nothing.

But I digress.

The worst problems in engineering teams are almost always over issues at an interface between sub teams, so that is what I focused on. Sub teams work pretty well within themselves. This is because engineers and developers communicate well with others who share their personal struggles and viewpoints.

Presented with information that contradicts their viewpoint, they will listen, if generally only to people they respect. If an engineer or developer doesn't respect you or see your value, they will ignore you. Subtly or otherwise.

Therefore, **I never disagree publicly with any technical person on a technical opinion they hold.** If they say that extra time is needed for a task, instead of disagreeing, I say to the rest of the team, *"You all are the experts. Where is this extra time coming from on the schedule?"*

As a team they had already agreed there was no slack (unused time) in the schedule we had created, so they would ultimately figure it out among the affected people. We never slipped a schedule done this way.

Meetings became useful in their minds. Imagine that!

"How to ultimately get to the finish line successfully."

CHAPTER NINE

Going from A to Z
Getting Successfully to the Finish Line

It always seems impossible until it's done.
–Nelson Mandela, 1st President of South Africa and activist

People will forget what you do, but never how you make them feel
– Maya Angelou, American memoirist, essayist, poet, and civil rights activist.

OK, hopefully you feel a bit better about your schedules, risk logs, metric management, team meetings, and monthly reviews. All of that. But how does all that fit into your day-to day-efforts, and how do you ultimately get to the finish line successfully?

"We've all heard that a new President's first 100 days in office often define the success or failure of their presidency. With team leadership in the tech world, I think you get about a month"

Your First Month or So

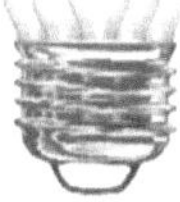

We've all heard that a new President's first 100 days in office often define the success or failure of their presidency. With team leadership in the tech world, I think you get about a month. You should use the approach below to make the most of that time.

This approach was refined by fits and starts over the years, based on the hard knocks and breakthroughs that occurred in the workplace jungle. I've used the approach many times.

To start, don't come in with guns a blazing telling everyone what is wrong with how they do things and then present your golden solution. Instead lay low for three weeks or so* as you ask several key questions in order to get to know the team's issues.

The Key Questions:

- What needs fixing around here?
- What works well?
- Is it a supportive, employee-oriented culture?
- Do you feel management has your back? (The last two questions weren't asked when the answer was obviously no)

When you come into your new project, obviously meet as many people as possible. Be sure to talk to the key team leaders, but other people as well. Schedule these meetings on their calendars for thirty minutes and be there on time and stop on time. Spread these meetings across a couple of weeks. That allows for the word to spread that "the new PM is different."

The team members should be talking around 85% of the time in these meetings, not you. Your main job is to listen, listen, listen! And then listen some more.

**With the exception being "You Can't Trust These People, You Know" in Chapter 7, a project with a six-week duration. There, I had about 30 minutes of time to lay low.

As you're asking the key questions, you want to also paraphrase back to them what they say; that is, you're testing for understanding. That builds rapport and trust. And, best of all, *you* learn.

Other questions should emerge organically as you talk. The conversation should be fun for both of you and seem to flow. At first, people may look at you skeptically and give you generic answers. That's understandable. But I have found, both in leadership roles and as an author, that people, when you show interest in them, love to talk about themselves, their lives, and their work.

About the second time someone gave me a non-answer answer, I would say something like, *"OK, I understand. You don't know me, you don't know what I'll do if you give me the straight story. I get that. So how about this,* ***I'll trust you to tell me the truth, if you trust me to tell you the truth. We'll do that until proven otherwise.****"*

I must have said that a couple hundred times over the years. It never ceased to gain me incredulous looks, generally followed a bit later by a relaxing of body language and, often a smile. They'd begun to trust me. And it almost always generated positive results.

When I didn't do this, like in "Zealot Failure" in Chapter 2, I never gained the trust of the team. We succeeded to our business goals, but I had no solid support from anyone within the team. Bad for me, bad for them. And I was removed. In all other projects mentioned in this book, I did some variation of the above (it got better over time) and my teams trusted me.

Introducing Your Approach at the All-Hands Meeting

Now that you know many of the key players and their thoughts on what is good and bad about how the organization and the team works, you are ready to roll out your findings and present your suggested approach. It is time for an all-hands team meeting.

You have to consider:

- What the team's maturity level is around changing the culture. Take change easy if you can, and gauge the approach to the team's maturity. You can be doing this last thing during your earlier interviews.
- More change may be required if there is a great deal of schedule time pressure.

The All-Hands meeting should be scheduled for one hour, and should naturally feel like ending five to ten minutes before the hour is up.

Items to introduce at the all-hands meeting:

- **The VIP VP.** If possible beforehand, invite the key leader in the building, generally the VP in charge. (See "An Accountable Senior Manager" in Chapter 3.) Have a meeting with her to cover what your plan is, and ask her to speak for a few minutes, amplifying your message. Because it is so rare, this taking of accountability by senior management will be taken seriously. They won't talk for long and will likely leave the meeting when they're done. That's just fine. It will help your credibility immensely if the team sees you being endorsed by such a VIP.

Next, you should personally speak to:

- **The key values and desired culture for the team**. On my projects these were always Integrity, Trust, Accountability, Communication, and Transparency. Sometimes I would have a slide on each concept, sometimes one bullet item per each concept. Anecdotes from the earlier chats with key team members might also be sprinkled in.

- **The team goal** that everyone would be working towards. For example, *"we need to ship a completed core eight months from today,"* or *"we need to have a stream-worthy website ready by the XYZ event in six weeks."*
- **A milestone schedule,** that is, one milestone every two weeks.
- **Approach to team meetings, risk management, metrics**, and any other key topic that might pertain.

You should cover the above items in about twenty minutes or so. Anywhere from four to seven slides. Any longer and you risk losing their interest.

Finally, the key developer or engineer should cover:

- The **technical requirements.** This approach shows everyone that the technical leaders are readily working with you. This detailed techie talk should not be allowed to go on forever. Leave plenty of time for questions.

Ongoing Leadership

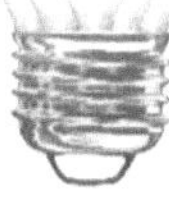

While the first month with your team is critical, it is of course only the start. Next you must build on your early success.

In the beginning, teams have high energy and motivation, and then use adrenaline to finish. But they often struggle in the middle of projects.

Senior management will often try to pressure a team to stay high on adrenaline for a whole project, but that really doesn't work. I told my teams if they were working more than 45 hours per week at a creative job, it probably was counterproductive. Meanwhile, many more senior managers were demanding more hours, honestly, sometimes as high as 100 hours per week. Crazy.

Here are some ideas that will help keep you and the team focused along the way.

- **Team Meetings** and 1:1s with key individuals. Assign action items and follow up on them for status.
- **Keep Good Meeting Minutes**. In this case you *are* a good secretary. I view it as doing my job to ensure issues are captured for the team. Without a good list of needed actions, the whole thing falls apart. If you don't do so, each sub-team will go their own way, polishing and repolishing their portion of the code until the inevitable disaster becomes obvious.
- **Agendas**. Publish the agenda of each meeting a few days before the meeting. Be clear and specific. Agenda items for team meetings should affect more than one sub-group. For issues involving just one sub-group, you can talk to them or their leader 1:1.
- **Risk Logs**. Develop a simple and easy to explain log of the key risks to the project's success. Part of the team meeting should update needed status on these items. The team should decide the risk, its intensity, and the needed action item. You track and follow up on all that and ensure proper discussion occurs.

- **Monthly Reviews**. Most organizations have their own formats for these reviews, but that doesn't mean you can't add a page or two. Current status of the schedule, risks, and the metrics the team cares about are what you should focus on while also answering the emails for what management specifically wants to know.

Even though senior management was supposed to be helpful, I rarely saw monthly reviews as an opportunity to ask for help. Action items assigned at those management meetings were rarely *effective* in helping the team.

Monthly reviews are simply too politically charged. Senior and departmental managers are better politicians than me or probably you. Along those lines, you always want to be on the staff of whomever the engineering manager reports to (direct line, not indirect). This is so you'll have a godfather speaking up for you in the rooms you're not in.

- Depending on the personality of the team, hand out some **rewards**. I rarely used this with development teams. With them, frequent pizza parties were effective. Rewards worked great with manufacturing teams. They weren't used to being noticed, so public recognition was awesome to them.
- Finally, always **listen for the undertone /sub-text /meaning between the lines of what people say**, not just the actual words. Listen closely for emerging problems. Your team leaders will tell you if you ask; hopefully even if you don't. Working level people will also tell you things, but you should always ask, "Have you talked about this with your supervisor?" This is so you don't knee cap the involved supervisor.

You should thank everyone and tell them that you are going to take what they tell you seriously. If the culture on the project is as it should be, no one will get beat up for raising problems. If this does occur, stand up to the issue by reminding everyone of the principles agreed to on the project.

At this point I still hear people say, *"my projects somehow still perform sub-optimally, or even fail. And it's just not my fault!"* I understand. You gotta get the right information. Here's how.

Asking the Right Questions

A good manager doesn't try to eliminate conflict; he tries to keep it from wasting the energies of his people.
—Robert Townsend, best-selling author and executive

A genuine leader is not a searcher for consensus, but a molder of consensus.
—Dr. Martin Luther King, Jr.

As Ajay C. says in Appendix B, *"Doug would sit in the meetings, listen carefully, get to the root cause of the issues, ask the right questions at the right time—and then help to guide us in the right direction."*

Another person quoted in the same document often asked me how I did that. I have thought quite a bit about this question and I just don't know. How does Anthony Edwards dunk a basketball? He doesn't analyze how; he just does it.

Our daughter calls skills that she can't explain "her superpowers." As good an explanation as anything, I guess.

The right question to ask depends on the situation. Here is my best explanation on how to ask the right questions.

As Ajay says above, what I am trying to get at is the root cause of the issue. What exactly does that mean for me, a person who—while an engineering graduate and a member of the electrical engineering honor society—is likely to be the person least expert technically in the room?

It means I am trying to dig out the viewpoints that are being put forward by the different factions in the room, who—if left to their own devices—would almost certainly not solve the issue, at least not without wasting a lot of time and angry energy, only to come up with a less effective solution.

I help the team process the viewpoints (it's usually two) being discussed in a way that is overall best for the team. The schedule is generally the number one priority and hence the hardest arguments revolve around schedules.

Everyone sees things their own way, that is, they would like a little schedule cushion for their tasks, or be able to do more checks on their code. But if they are in a culture of *"delivering a quality product when we say we will,"* they can overlook their parochial interests for the benefit of the team.

This circumstance of two groups arguing equally valid positions until they are blue in the face is exactly why there are no buffers in my schedules. It puts everyone up against a hard fact: no wiggle room.

In that way, you enable the team to confront a statement from a team member, such as: *"We have to do this. It'll take my sub-team two extra weeks."* I never argue with these statements. They are the technical experts.

I simply reply, *"Fine. There is no buffer in our schedule, as we have repeatedly agreed and told everyone."* Nods from around the room. Needless to say, telling management you are going to slip one of their critical projects is not something for the faint of heart. Or the career minded. That is why the need to slip is often "hidden" and not brought up to management. It is better to work the issue out thus protecting the schedule.

I'll say, *"So, if this work has to be done and it adds two weeks, do we need to go to management and tell them we are going to slip?"* This often causes the two factions to look at each other and say something like, *"No, we'll figure it out."* **That in a nutshell is "why" I ask these questions.**

They then generally adjust—not so much the scope of the work itself—but how they can creatively meet the scope in the original time. They work together!

This is driven by desperate need and knowing more about the work at that later date than when the tasks were first estimated. Thus, it is possible—without sandbagging the original schedule—to get the same work done in a more efficient manner than initially estimated. Also, teams, when planning, sometimes include extra "nice to have" tasks that can be dropped later with no risk. Extra testing, things of that sort. Engineers are risk averse, and will sometimes add tasks not absolutely needed. Perfectionism, remember?

Cost is also generally an important part of these discussions. And if the decision is made to add people to the team, I always ask questions like *"who might they be, where are they going to come from, and how do we get them spun up quickly."* Experienced senior engineers are very good at answering these questions.

Finally, it should go without saying that we never trade off quality.

In any meeting, but particularly a team meeting, as I wrote above, I am always **listening to the tone of what is being said.** Technical people are almost always honest when asked a direct question. However, they answer from the perspective of their experience and specialty, and that can make things tricky.

Also, their answers are almost always too detailed, and sometimes somewhat inarticulate. The tone of their statements alerts me that this might be *"one of those discussion points"* where I need to jump in.

This active listening requires:

- Practice in the soft skills.
- Experience, as engineering problems across industries and applications have similarities.
- Empathy in order to see everyone's viewpoint from *their* perspective; and
- A fair amount of articulateness to capture and repeat clearly what each side is saying. Always make sure they agree you are fairly restating what they've said.

This sets up "getting at the root causes." Now that there are two clearly stated viewpoints, stated by an independent person (you), questions spin off naturally from the two statements. In that way, the technically smart and talented people in the room will almost always get to an acceptable way of "Doing this without a schedule slip." The result, as Ajay said, *"gets us to where we need to be."*

Make sense? Now go for it!

"Follow this process and you will almost certainly have a list of what needs fixing that is longer and more useful than you thought possible."

Finding Out What's Wrong

I doubt you will come into a team or project that has no problems. If so, great, I guess. In that case, I'm not sure this book is for you. Your situation is either too easy or this approach doesn't make sense for your application.

To find what's wrong when you come into a project:

- Stay below the radar early. Don't make waves or throw your opinions around. You're in the "intelligence gathering and trust building mode," not the "I'm the expert, y'all shut up and listen," mode.

Three ways to capture needed actions:

- If someone, in hallway conversation, says something like, *"Well here he or she is, I hear you're going to fix things around here!"* Your reply is not your own opinion, or to be snide like them, but to ask the question, "What do *you* think needs fixing?"
- One-on-ones with key team members and leaders within the first couple of weeks, and with anyone else they might suggest for those things they don't have all the detail on.
- Team meetings, of course. The action associated with problem solving, a meeting!

Also:

- Listen with feeling (see "Well and Truly Listen" in Chapter 4). That means you must care about what you hear, not just act as if you care. If you don't care, people will parse that out. Mirror back what you hear. Make sure they agree, or rephrase until they agree.
- You have to write down the essentials of what you hear. Carry a pad around with you at all times, maybe in your pocket like I now do to capture book thoughts and ideas. In meetings, of course you can use your computer or pad.

- You must capture the issue, action item, person responsible, and due date.
- Follow up with the responsible person before the due date. Update as needed. Push until that action is finished.
- Publish the current list of "actions being worked on."

Follow this process and you will almost certainly have a list of what needs fixing that is longer and more useful than you thought possible.

How to Fix What's Wrong

Remember, you are there to help the team succeed while also meeting the organization's goals. When the team sees this as your only agenda item, trust will grow. Even skeptics may begin to bring up issues as they see your approach take root and results begin to benefit the team.

To fix problems:

- Remember it won't happen in a day. But, if you can break the inertia so that problems are being discussed, you are moving the culture forward. Stay positive.
- Hold yourself accountable as you try to hold others accountable for their action items.
- Be patient, but firm. Always be direct, specific, and non-punishing in your communications.
- Problem-solving data gathering can be also be done by you 1:1 with the accountable person. The conversation can be low key, nothing formal. Seeing them in the hall or stopping by their cube can work.
- Call small meetings of 2 or 3 involved parties for issues that involve their areas. Match the problem solving in groups or team meetings to those problems that affect the group in the meeting. This is to deal with problems like those mentioned in the Chapter 5 story "Little Endian: Sorting the Wheat from the Chaff."
- Try to have a senior manager or a VP agree to help fix problems you or the team leader can't.
- Hold everyone equally accountable. Even VPs. If they won't cooperate ask them who would be better. If they sarcastically say, *"You! That's why we brought you in,"* reply the appropriate part of: *"The team has identified this as an issue only you can help with. I don't have the horsepower / brains / connections you have. Maybe you could email or call your equivalent at the vendor/ other team/ corporate expert to*

ask for help and hand it back to me or the development leader after that." Appeal to their pride /ego /desire to help, as applicable.

- Publish the results and highlight important solutions at the monthly project reviews. If the standard format doesn't allow for it, put an extra page of your own in that shows big successes. Give credit where due to those who cooperated.
- Realize everyone is noticing everything you say and do, including your body language, all the time.
- Stay with it. Make this list one of the key tasks you drive.
- Go back to top of this list and repeat.

I am sure you, your team, and management will ultimately be glad for the results you lead the team to.

Seventh Inning Stretch
Shifting Gears before the Race to the Finish Line

This story deals with how you modify your approach as you enter the end game. I coined the term "seventh inning stretch" when working with a huge baseball fan who was also a great engineering manager. (In fact, after all these years, he still has my complete set of the PBS "Baseball" series.) I explained, *"A baseball manager changes how he manages near the end of the game, right?"* He got the point immediately.

Not only at that point in the project is there less work left but there is almost no time to recover if there are problems, so problems have to be identified and fixed very quickly. The team and you are tired, but your focus *can* tighten and your intensity can increase.

You should do these specific things:

- Start daily fifteen-minute stand-ups, deemphasizing the importance of the weekly team meetings, which should still be held.
- Add detail to the remaining schedule items. Identify the critical path and manage to it, but also watch other remaining tasks like a hawk.
- As there are now fewer risks, you should scrutinize and drive risk mitigation even harder than before.
- Stop tracking action items and risks that don't affect the remaining tasks and ship date.
- Metrics as early warning devices don't work well now, so at this point they honestly aren't much good. Use them for what you find useful.
- Discuss whether adding a few of the right people—emphasis on the word few—would improve the odds of hitting the end date. The team leaders, who will manage these people, should make these decisions, with you asking the right confirming questions.

As you approach the finish line, double and triple check everything. Your fifteen-minute morning stand-ups should be the most important meetings of the day.

When you ship on or ahead of schedule have a celebration! Pizza's on me!

In conclusion, I am one lucky dude, able to meet my desire for new challenges every 18 months or so. The experience from a 35-year plus career allows me to see across a huge landscape. I experienced many emotions, but I was almost never bored, and hardly ever dreaded going to work.

I leave you with a quote from Usain Bolt, the eight-time Olympic gold medalist sprinter, "*Kill them with success and bury them with a smile.*"

I hope you've enjoyed this book and will find it useful.

APPENDICES

Success with both Projects and Teams

APPENDIX A

MAJOR SUCCESSFUL PROJECTS

[Both Business and People Success]

Manufacturing (6)

1. Led complex $100K per unit product from development into production.

2-5. "Focused Factory" of four products with same team. One project achieved six sigma quality.

6. Microwave Products Factory 35-person operations team. Increased throughput over 65% in 6 mos.

Engineering Systems Development (4)

7-8. Led cross-corporate joint venture for two new products created on-time and within spec over 15 -month period.

9. Restructured engineering operations in small defense contractor, including changing IT, test, and development from functional to small integrated teams.

10. Introduced cross-functional high-performance work team concept for rugged radio/computer manpack system for US Army.

Software Development (10)

11. Led development team for successful worldwide streaming event despite extremely short six-week schedule

12-18. Seven consecutive critical microprocessor cores delivered on-time

19. Changed culture and led project management team in microprocessor development team for a different corporation.

20. Reduced manpower required by 40% over 8-month period for equivalent software work versus previous effort.

Failures

21. Zealot Failure (business success; people failure)

20.5/21project success rate=97.6%

APPENDIX B

WHAT OTHERS ARE SAYING ABOUT DOUG

[Quotes Provided to Doug by Others Over the Years]

Ajay C. CAD Manager, Nvidia Corporation

"Doug is the most amazing program manager that I have ever had the pleasure of working with. He is a fabulous leader. *He is, without a doubt, the greatest mentor that I've had during my career. I learned more from working with Doug in 2 yrs than I've learned from anyone else. I managed a small team of 4 engineers who were responsible for a test chip and for integration and delivery of IP used in systems-on-chip designs. Doug was the program manager for all of the projects that I worked on while I was in a particular area.*

Doug worked with about 8 different design managers in our group. The managers each had varying levels of management experience. Design managers often keep two sets of books: an internal schedule that they strive towards and an external schedule for everyone else. This tendency leads to trust issues and communication problems between groups. The problem is that most engineering managers have never had the opportunity to learn the skills necessary to become great managers. You learn these skills by example from people like Doug Russell. Doug would sit in the meetings, listen carefully, get to the root cause of the issues, ask the right questions at the right time—and then help to guide us in the right direction. ***Doug taught us to listen to each other, to trust one another.*** *Everyone has the ability to be great. Doug is able to bring out that greatness in those around him."*

John A. Microprocessor Design Manager and Freescale Semiconductor Corporation Fellow, currently AMD VP

"My initial engagement with Doug was when he was at Motorola as a Program Manager and manager of the Program Management Office. I knew the management process of doing designs was broke.

In those few years, Doug was crucial to training the team. *He was skilled at building schedules, managing risks and issues, and building solid* *mitigation plans. He managed a team of Program Managers that enabled multiple successful projects. I have recently worked with Doug as an* **executive coach**. *Doug worked with me with evaluating my team as well as my own overall strengths, and then we worked on how to best leverage those strengths for the team's overall success. Doug helped me do some self-evaluations and worked through some problem solving on existing issues or situations inside the organization. Overall, Doug is a great listener and coach. He is capable of taking difficult problems and breaking them down to their root cause. As a coach, Doug kept me focused on my overall goals and helped me better understand myself and my aspirations. Project Management improved the groups' communication, and helped us deal with our unknowns up-front, and we managed the risks."*

Keith K. Director, Corporate Program Management Office, Major Semiconductor Corporation

"I have personally witnessed Doug Russell turn around a dysfunctional team to a 'well-oiled machine' *contributing to the flawless execution of a flagship product for the corporation. People are having fun driving great results because of Doug's balanced coaching approach."*

Bob B. An Internal Customer

"What impressed me most in the beginning was the way they committed to what they were going to do and then they stayed with it. Never wavered, even under the pressure of management to further 'pull in' their schedules."

Larry M. Physical Design Manager (Layout)

"I was tired of being crunched for time at the end of the projects because the front-end design teams continued to try to make their designs perfect. I was ready to try something new."

Jeff G. Web Designer, Start-Up

"I really enjoyed the time I had working with you. You were the best thing to happen to us in regards to bringing the individual departments together to actually function as a team and stay on schedule".

Brian B. Director, Engineering Design Manager

"When I took on the role of Design Manager for a team of 60 some odd semiconductor design engineers, I was more or less like one of them, that is I thought and behaved like an engineer, in the sense that circuits and invention and simulations were more important to me (and us) than meeting commitments.

Not long after, Doug was hired to inject what I now call 'professional PM' skills into our team, and drive us to plan, execute, track, mitigate and ultimately deliver on our promises. **It would be an understatement to say that the team was skeptical of—in their words—having to do 'extra' work, but Doug partnered with the team and myself quite successfully to convince them that indeed, acting with a PM mindset was not extra work, it simply was the work.** *In the end, the team rallied around this new way of working, reinforced by the positive feedback they started receiving when their results not only met the stringent technical requirements, but also were also predictable in schedule and cost.*

Through this transformation, Doug was able to reinforce the 'what' and 'how' of the new methods, but also the 'why', which was instrumental in seeing the transformation through to a successful conclusion. I can state without a doubt that this was a watermark experience for me in my young management career, and I have driven many successful projects since that time using these tried-and-true principles across large, complex organizations."

John S. Design Integration Leader

(An early resister*) "The design groups had a tendency in the past to continue to 'tweak' their designs and not finish, paying little attention to the overall schedule."* I thought to myself, *'This time there's going to be schedule accountability from the start.' The greatest thing was the many fewer late nights and a lot less overtime and worry."*

Sasi B. Enterprise Architect, Semiconductor Corporation

"*Working with Doug was a very positive experience for me. My observations were that* **as lead of the Risk Management Core Team, which managed and governed the methodology and tools for the corporate platform office, Doug had to deal with a wide range and variety of customers and he executed flawlessly.** *His people skills and logical reasoning in addition to his technical knowledge exceeded expectations, which contributed well to success of the mission of the team."*

Mark K. State Farm Insurance Agent, Devine TX

"Doug is a thought partner for me. *To have someone who understands what I have to do [as a leader] and has the courage to challenge me to get there is great!"*

Bob C. former Operations Section Manager, author in the field of Organizational Design

"I hired Doug Russell as an assistant Project Leader upon his receiving his MBA degree from Duke University. He quickly became one of my most important, and successful, champions of the High-Performance Productions Teams that I was attempting to establish. Later as a Program Manager, ***Doug was instrumental in the creation of our first High Performance Engineering Design team."***

Mike C. Senior Staff Engineer, Major Semiconductor Company

"I learned a lot from Doug about building teams of engineers. ***He gets very individualistic engineers to work together by listening to their concerns but being firm about what the organization needs. I was amazed.*** *Doug's coaching has been invaluable in helping me to articulate what is important to me as I move into the next phase of my career. He got me to drop my narrow focus on past accomplishments to see other areas in which I could apply my skills."*

Bill L Previously Director, Major Semiconductor Company

"Doug has an intense passion to see his team succeed, and invests himself entirely to see that happen as a part of any team he is on. ***He loves to work with groups focused on a common purpose,*** *giving direction and coaching oriented to the needed outcome. Doug and I worked together on several teams, ranging from 20 to 50 engineers, within a larger organization working to deliver multiple projects on time and with first-time success. He was instrumental in helping each team achieve their goals by bringing a new level of discipline and focus. I highly recommend Doug to any team needing to move to the next level of accomplishment."*

Jahnara A. Project Analyst, Major Semiconductor Corporation

" *I had the pleasure of knowing Doug Russell as my manager for almost one year. Doug was highly respected by his team. Many of his co-workers sought his advice and support. Doug was always there for them and his enthusiasm and dedication was very inspiring and motivating.* ***His interpersonal and communication skills have allowed him to develop productive working relationships with both our clients and our staff."***

Thomas P. Sub-module Team Leader

"*In the past we weren't focused as a team. As I listened to what Brian and Doug were saying,* ***I hoped two things would occur.*** *First, Project Management would bring us together as a team, and two, that it would provide a consistent set of expectations across the sub-teams.*

I was better able to explain to my team what we were trying to achieve. This allowed us to consider more than just pure design issues."

Doug's Thought Process?

APPENDIX C

THE BRIEFEST OF CHECKLISTS

1. Even though this is a short 51,443-word book, there are many thoughts and statements to process. This checklist is basically the thought process I go through.

2. Continuously educate yourself on best practices by reading, taking courses, networking, attending IEEE, PMI and like organizations.

3. Apply those best practices in a transparent (clear and open) way.

4. Use 1:1s to get to know your team. Share some of your approach in those conversations and draw out their thoughts. Use what you learn to fine tune your approach so that it matches your team.

5. State the team goals in front of the entire team and senior management.

6. Hold yourself and the team accountable for what is agreed to.

7. Use simple metrics and a risk log, and maybe earned Value, to measure performance to key project goals.

8. Give the team useful feedback on schedule, metric, and risk management performance. Track, communicate, and drive action items that help the team met its goals.

9. Use near-term milestones as your scheduling focus. This enables the team to relax into their work and not focus on the end date.

10. Delegate everything possible—except responsibility—down to the organization where the work will be performed.

11. Do all of this in a positive and supportive culture that assumes the best of everyone until proven otherwise.

APPENDIX D

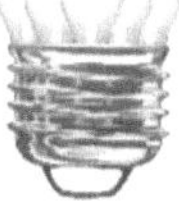

DICTIONARY OF DOUGISMS

Some of Doug's catchphrases known as *Dougisms*, but don't deserve more than a sentence or two to explain. They follow.

Bring Me a Rock: A toxic management technique where, no matter what information (rock) you give them, they (management) don't think it's good enough and send you back to find more data (another rock).

Come to Jesus Meeting: Used for motivation. A not-so-polite way of pointing out your dissatisfaction with a situation in order to try to get on the same page. Can be 1:1 or multi-to-one or one-to-multi.

Day Jail: Describes the opposite of how we want our teams to feel about their jobs.

Direct, Specific, and Non-punishing: How we want to communicate. For example: *"The problem is that Tool Zeta doesn't work as advertised, and we need to identify who is going to take point on this issue."* I was exposed to this concept in a course at Motorola University.

Drawing a Line in the Sand: An effort to create boundaries that often is about as easy to do as keeping sand from shifting in the winds. Not meant to be a positive.

Drinking Your Own Bathwater: Used to prevent hubris. Feeling really good about yourself for no good reason. Fooling yourself. In a team context, it becomes **drinking our own bathwater**.

Fire Drill Mindset: A technique used to get noticed in a dysfunctional culture where a person creates non-existent problems and then solves them. Often a path to success in those organizations.

Fireside Chat: Used for motivation. A conversation to politely show someone the error of their ways. Almost always used as a 1:1.

Godfather: Your Key Ally in senior+ management. Someone higher than you in the org with sufficient clout to protect your interests when you're not in the room. Gotta' have a godfather (or godmother)!

High-Performing Team: Desired state within the team. Everybody is doing a useful role, there is a culture of continuous improvement, and the team is on a path to meet its goals.

I Can P*ss Higher on the Wall Than You: A bullying technique of poor management. Used when the person doesn't know what else to do, it is much akin to how alpha males in herd species, such as bison or musk oxen, try to impress and dominate each other.

Informative Meeting: Sharing news with the team considering their frame of reference, and not your chance to play big boss. You will probably talk the most at this meeting, but watch the audience for questions and leave plenty of time for Q&A.

Management Shill. Survival mechanism for the clueless and incompetent. Managers and others who find out the "management desire of the day" and cater to it. Team members quickly suss out these folks and ignore or minimize them.

Non-Maskable Interrupt. A geeky, but nevertheless apt, term for a critical situation that must be dealt with immediately. Not to be confused in any way with the response to a "Fire Drill."

Rope A Dope. A technique for not doing what you've been asked to do by never letting the other person get to the ask. Different from saluting the flag; salute-the-flaggers give the impression they are on board. See "Dealing with Odd Ducks" in Chapter five.

Saluting The Flag. When someone acts like they heard what you asked them to do without the intention of ever doing it, but without telling you so.

Senior Management. Anyone higher in the organization than you, no matter the department. To some people, you may appear to be senior management, which is generally not a good thing for you.

Seventh-Inning-Stretch Type Stand-Up Meetings. A coordination meeting near the end of the project. Only impediments to project finish are brought up. Read about this in the story by the same name in Chapter 9.

Smartest-guy-in-the-room Syndrome. The arrogance often displayed by smart and well-educated engineers or managers who don't know what they don't know and aren't interested in learning.

Trust and Expect to be Trusted. How to comport yourself at all times with your fellow team members.

Two-Armed Salute. A deflection technique endemic at one place I worked. Describes a situation where no one is accountable, and multiple people point at different other people as responsible. See the story of the same name in Chapter 6.

Who's On First? A deflection technique derived from the famous Abbott & Costello sketch. Used to describe a situation so messed up that it's hard to tell exactly what the problem is and how to fix it.

"An Alphabetical List of Sources"

APPENDIX D

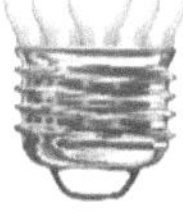

BIBLIOGRAPHY

BOOKS

Barnes, John A. *Ulysses S. Grant on Leadership.* Roseville, CA: Prima Forum, 2001.

Bennis, Warren and Daniel Goleman and James O'Toole with Patricia Ward Biderman. *Transparency: How Leaders Create a Culture of Candor.* New York: Jossey-Bass, 2008.

Cain, Susan. *Quiet: The Power of Introverts in a World That Can't Stop Talking.* New York: Crown Publishers, 2012.

Cobb, Ervin (Earl). *Becoming Transformational Leaders In The Post-Biden Era: Leveraging Visioning, Veracity and Vocalization.* Savannah, Ga: RICHER Press, 2025.

Cobb, Ervin (Earl) and Charlotte D. Grant-Cobb, *Living a More Thoughtful Life: Thinkable Thoughts and Relevant Reflections.* Savannah, Ga: RICHER Press, 2022.

Covey, Stephen R. *Principle-Centered Leadership.* New York: Simon and Schuster, 1991.

Damasio, Antonio. *Descartes' Error, Emotion, Reason, and the Human Brain.* New York: Penguin Books, 2005.

Goleman, Daniel. *Emotional Intelligence: Why It Can Matter More than IQ.* New York: Random House, 2005.

Goodwin, Doris Kearns. *Leadership in Turbulent Times.* New York: Simon and Schuster, 2021.

Graebner, David. *Bullshit Jobs: A Theory.* New York: Simon and Schuster, 2018.

Hateley, Barbara and Warren H. Schmidt. *A Peacock in the Land of the Penguins: A Tale of Diversity and Discovery.* San Francisco: Berrett-Koehler, 1997

Hesselbein, Frances. *Hesselbein on Leadership.* San Francisco: Jossey-Bass, 2002.

Hughes, Marcia, and James Bradford Terrell. *The Emotionally Intelligent Team: Understanding and Developing the Behaviors of Success.* San Francisco: Jossey-Bass. 2007.

Joiner, Brian L. *Fourth Generation Management: The New Business Consciousness.* New York: McGraw Hill,1984.

Keirsey, David and Marilyn Bates. *Please Understand Me: Character and Temperament Types.* Del Mar, CA: Prometheus Nemesis, 1984.

Krzyzewski, Mike. *Leading with the Heart: Coach K's Successful Strategies for Basketball, Business and Life.* With Donald T Phillips. New York: Warner Books, 2001. *The Gold Standard: Building a World Class Team.* With Jamie K. Spatola. New York: Business Plan, 2009.

Russell, Doug. *Succeeding in the Project Management Jungle: How to Manage the People Side of Projects.* New York: American Management Association, 2011.

Wooden, John. *Wooden: A Lifetime of Observations and Reflections On and Off the Court.* With Steve Jamison. New York: McGraw Hill, 1997.

Townsend, Robert. *Up the Organization: How to Stop the Corporation from Stifling People and Strangling Profit.* San Francisco: Jossey-Bass, 2007.

Walker III, Dr. Joseph W. *Leadership & Loneliness.* Nashville: Zion Publishing, 2021.

Internet

Myriad websites for leadership quotes.
Schwartz, Brenna. *The Risk Management Process in Project Management* (www.projectmanager.com/blog/risk-management-process-steps).2025.

White, Bradford Morgan. "Abort Retry Fail," post on Substack.
World Metrics Organization.org. Data on improvement process costs.

ABOUT THE AUTHOR

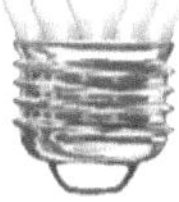

Doug Russell lives in Virginia with his wife, one lazy dog, one cracked cat, and one sly and crafty cat. Three children are strewn around the country and now the world. Doug earned a Master's Degree in Business Administration (MBA) from Duke University and a Bachelor's Degree in Electrical and Computer Engineering from Clemson University. This is his third published book.

He has over 30-years of Technical, Project Management and Leadership experience with major U.S. Corporations, such as Intel and Motorola, and has held major Project Leadership responsibilities with the United States Department of Defense.

Other Books by Doug Russell

Project and Technical Teams

Many of the books on the leadership shelves are high-level and written by non-engineers, people who weren't present on the tech battlefield if you will. Thus, the anecdotes are often not their own. In other words, they weren't involved in the ongoing day-to-day process of making it happen. That's where I come in. I've been there...And in this book, share it all with you.

www.ingramcontent.com/pod-product-compliance
Lightning Source LLC
LaVergne TN
LVHW090558110826
845146LV00001B/175

9798992899658